83084

D0843002

An Intelligent Person's Guide to Modern Culture

An Intelligent Person's Guide to Modern Culture

Roger Scruton

ST. AUGUSTINE'S PRESS
South Bend, Indiana
2000

Manufactured in the United States of America.

1 2 3 4 5 6   07 06 05 04 03 02 01 00

Library of Congress Cataloging in Publication Data
Scruton, Roger.
    An intelligent person's guide to modern culture / Roger
      Scruton.
        p. cm.
    Includes bibliographical references and index.
    ISBN 1-890318-47-7 (alk. paper)
      1. Culture. 2. Arts, Modern. 3. Civilization, Modern –
Philosophy. 4. Popular culture. I. Title.

HM621.S27 2000
306 – dc21   00-027225

What remains when disbelief is gone?
Philip Larkin, 'Church going'.

Contents

Preface to the American Edition

The English edition of this book was criticised for making so little mention of photography, cinema and TV. How can you write about modern culture, I was asked, if you say nothing about the most striking cultural invention of our times? I have therefore added a short chapter on the photographic image, in order to show how. I have even found something to say about television, and if I went on in this vein I could include a learned disquisition on junk food, baseball caps and chrome-plated Cadillacs. There are plenty of works on modern culture which attend to such things, indiscriminately rejoicing in every fashion or fad that could conceivably be given 'cultural' credentials. But my purpose is not theirs: I wish to explain what culture is, and why it matters. I have therefore concentrated on philosophical questions concerning the moral life and the significance of our social emotions.

These questions are, it seems to me, vital to the future of what used to be called humane or liberal education – the education of the emotions through the study of history, literature and art. We read of 'culture wars' in the American academy, with radicals ranged against traditionalists in a battle for the curriculum and for the minds and souls of the young. If we are to make sense of these wars, and to know whether they are the real thing or just a game, we need to study what culture is, how it is transmitted, and what it does to those who receive it. That is the purpose of this book.

Malmesbury, 2000

Preface

This book presents a theory of modern culture, and a defence of culture in its higher and more critical form. It is impossible to give a convincing defence of high culture to a person who has none. In the following book I shall therefore assume that you, the reader, are both intelligent and cultivated. You don't have to be familiar with the entire canon of Western literature, the full range of musical and artistic masterpieces or the critical reflections which all these things have prompted. Who is? But it would be useful to have read *Les fleurs du mal* by Baudelaire and T.S. Eliot's *Waste Land*. I shall also assume some familiarity with Mozart, Wagner, Manet, Poussin, Tennyson, Schoenberg, George Herbert, Goethe, Marx and Nietzsche. In Chapters 6 and 7 I offer criticisms of two important cultural figures – Michel Foucault and Jacques Derrida. I have tried, though perhaps without success, to make these criticisms intelligible to people who have not read, and maybe do not intend to read, Foucault or Derrida.

Culture, I suggest, has a religious root and a religious meaning. This does not mean that you have to be religious in order to be cultivated. But it does mean that the point of being cultivated cannot, in the end, be explained without reference to the nature and value of religion. That suggestion is controversial; to many people it will seem absurd. Moreover, I have found no conclusive argument in support of it, but only avenues of speculation and associative thought. My consolation, in considering the inadequacy of what I have written, is that every other attempt I have come across is just as bad.

What follows would have been even worse, however, were it not for criticisms and suggestions offered by Fiona Ellis, Bob Grant, Jim Johnson, and David Wiggins, and I am greatly indebted to all of them. I am also indebted to the University College of Swansea, for inviting me to give the J.R. Jones Memorial Lecture in 1993, some of the material from which has been recycled in Chapter 11, to the Nexus Institute at the University of Tilburg in the Netherlands, for inviting me to take part in two conferences, one on Wagner and the other on idolatry, so inspiring the argument of Chapters 6 and 7, to the Trustees of the Peter Fuller Memorial Trust for inviting me to give the 1995 Peter Fuller Memorial Lecture, which has been reprocessed, rectified and reneged upon in Chapter 8, and to the University of Cambridge, for inviting me to deliver the Leslie Stephen Memorial Lecture in 1997, so launching me on the path which led to Chapter 9. A part of this last chapter has appeared in *City Journal,* and I am grateful to the editor of that journal, Myron Magnet, for permission to re-use the material.

Malmesbury, Summer 1998

1
What Is Culture?

The concept of culture leapt fully armed from the head of Johann Gottfried Herder in the mid-eighteenth century, and has been embroiled in battles ever since. *Kultur,* for Herder, is the life-blood of a people, the flow of moral energy that holds society intact. *Zivilisation*, by contrast, is the veneer of manners, law and technical know-how. Nations may share a civilisation; but they will always be distinct in their culture, since culture defines what they are.

This idea developed in two directions. The German romantics (Schelling, Schiller, Fichte, Hegel, Hölderlin) construed culture in Herder's way, as the defining essence of a nation, a shared spiritual force which is manifest in all the customs, beliefs and practices of a people. Culture, they held, shapes language, art, religion and history, and leaves its stamp on the smallest event. No member of society, however ill-educated, is deprived of culture, since culture and social membership are the same idea.

Others, more classical than romantic, interpreted the word in its Latin meaning. For Wilhelm von Humboldt, founding father of the modern university, culture meant not untended growth but *cultivation*. Not everyone possesses it, since not everyone has the leisure, the inclination or the ability to learn what is needed. And among cultivated people, some are more cultivated than others. The purpose of a university is to preserve and enhance the cultural inheritance, and to impart it to the next generation.

The two ideas are still with us. The early anthropologists adopted Herder's conception, and wrote of culture as the practices and beliefs which form the self-identity of a tribe. Every member of the tribe possesses the culture, since this is what membership requires. Matthew Arnold and the literary critics whom he influenced (including Eliot, Leavis and Pound) followed Humboldt, in treating culture as the property of an educated elite, an attainment which involves intellect and study.

To avoid confusion, I shall distinguish 'common culture', which is what the anthropologist describes, from 'high culture', which is a form of expertise. This purely negative distinction does not tell us what high culture is, whether it is one thing or many, or whether it is the great value that Arnold and his followers have assumed it to be. Obviously, therefore, I must return to such questions; and the necessity is all the greater in that, unlike most people I encounter, I agree with Matthew Arnold. It is my view that the high culture of our civilisation contains knowledge which is far more significant than anything that can be absorbed from the channels of popular communication. This is a hard belief to justify, and a harder one to live with; indeed, it has nothing to recommend it apart from its truth.

Those two concepts of culture have been embroiled in controversy throughout modern times. From the debris of their many battles has grown a third conception. The 'common culture' of a tribe is a sign of its inner cohesion. But tribes are vanishing from the modern world, as are all forms of traditional society. Customs, practices, festivals, rituals and beliefs have acquired a fluid and half-hearted quality which reflects our nomadic and rootless existence, predicated as we are on the global air-waves. Despite this, and despite all the conveniences and labour-saving devices that make other people more dispensable, modern city dwellers are as much social beings as were traditional tribesmen. They are unable to live in peace until furnished with a social identity, an outward garb which, by representing them to others, gives them confidence in themselves. This search for 'identity' pervades modern life. Although it is a fluid thing, and may change direction several times in a lifetime, or even twice in a year, it has much in common with the tribesman's attachment to a common culture. The cultivation of 'identity' is a mode of 'being-for-others', to use the existentialist jargon, a way of claiming space in a public world. At the same time it is founded in choice, taste and leisure; it is fed on popular art and entertainment; in broadest terms, it is a work of the imagination. In those respects it resembles the high culture of a literary and artistic tradition.

This third conception of culture – popular culture, as I shall call it – has become a familiar theme of sociology. It defines the subject-matter of 'cultural studies' – an academic discipline founded by Raymond Williams with a view to replacing academic English. Williams was a literary critic; but his egalitarian sympathies caused him to rebel against the elitist tradition in literary scholarship. Alongside the elite culture of the upper classes, he argued, there has always been another, by no means inferior, culture of the people, through which they affirmed their solidarity in the face of oppression and through which they expressed their social identity and their sense of belonging. Williams's anti-elitism struck a chord, and the concept of culture was extended to describe the forms of popular art and entertainment in modern conditions. As a result of this academic broadening, the concept began to lose its specificity. Any activity or artefact is considered cultural, if it is an identity-forming product of social interaction.

Popular culture is of two kinds: inherited and acquired. Globalisation has led to the extinction of the inherited (folk) cultures of Europe and America, and their replacement by the commercialised mish-mash that I discuss in later chapters. Some parts of folk culture – notably the music – became the raw material for high art, reappearing in transfigured form in Bartók, Vaughan Williams, and Copland. The rest changed its character from inherited tradition to commercialised 'heritage', and now stares from glass cases in the folk museum. Modern people may be charmed by folk costumes, folk dancing and folk festivals; but they do not find their identity through these things – which is another way of saying that folk culture is dead. 'Folk' is now a style within pop music, but one without roots in an inherited community.

Herder's idea of culture is 'particularist'. A culture is defined as something separate – an island of 'we' in the ocean of 'they'. Humboldt's conception is 'universalist': the cultivated person, for Humboldt, sees mankind as a whole, knows the art and literature of other peoples, and sympathises with human life in all its higher forms and aspirations. Why use the same word for two such conflicting ideas? Why write a book about culture, which treats 'common culture' and 'high culture' as though they were in some deep way connected? As an educated person I sympathise with Humboldt and Matthew Arnold. As an old-fashioned Englishman I lean towards Herder. One of my motives for writing this book is a sense that these two sympathies are fed from a common source.

Nevertheless, we must begin from the assumption that in discussing culture we are dealing with three or more distinct ideas. If you ask a simple question such as 'is toothpaste part of culture?' then Herder would say 'definitely not, though maybe it is a part of civilisation'. Arnold would also say no, adding, however, that the toothpaste deployed by Pam Germ in her prize-winning 'Portrait of a tape-worm' is part, though perhaps a regrettable part, of the national culture. The professor of cultural studies will probably reply 'of course tooth paste is a part of culture', since after all toothpaste is a way in which people form and express their social identity and the decision to use or not to use it is a decision directed towards others. (Imagine America without toothpaste!)

My method in what follows might be called archaeological. I shall be exploring strata in the modern consciousness, some very ancient and geological, some more recently deposited and still fermenting. I shall begin by considering common culture, and its place in the life of a tribe. Maybe it is eccentric to begin from this point; but it is also eccentric to begin from any other. For those who typically write about culture seldom begin. In the literature that I have come across, writers tend to start *in mediis rebus*, fighting on one side or another in battles which are now so confused that hardly anyone understands their meaning. And this is not because they do not see the wood for the trees, but because they have not dug beneath the trees, to the life which secretly feeds them.

2
Culture and Cult

The core of common culture is religion. Tribes survive and flourish because they have gods, who fuse the many wills into a single will, and demand and reward the sacrifices on which social life depends. Prayer is insufficient tribute to a genuine deity, who usually requires religious observance, in the form of ritual and sacrifice. There are many kinds of observance; but in our tradition – the tradition which includes Hellenic, Judaic and Christian cults, and which grew first in the fertile shores of the Mediterranean – we can discern an interesting pattern.

First, there is the community – the collective 'we' of dwelling and belonging, the social organism which thrives and suffers as one. The community (or a unified part of it) congregates at the shrine, and undertakes there a collective act, whereby the experience of membership is rehearsed and renewed.

Second, imposed upon and discovered in the feeling of community is the experience of pollution, separation or 'fall': the individual's sense, in the midst of the collective, that he is nevertheless in some way cast out and excluded, through some fault for which he must atone. Sometimes this is a moral fault – in other words, a crime that would be recognised as such even without the benefit of a religious perspective. Often, however, the religion that cures the fault also creates it – as with the Greek *miasma*, or with the pollution that comes from eating some forbidden animal, or with the idea of 'original sin' (i.e. a fault which is mine by nature and inescapable). Many who come to the shrine have no other fault than the original one – the 'crime of existence itself', as Schopenhauer puts it. But all have lived through the temptations for which the ritual atones.

Third, there follows an act of sacrifice, which is the primary ingredient in the process of atonement. Something is 'offered' at the altar, though not necessarily to anyone in particular; and this offering is a custom, regularly repeated, and framed by ceremonial gestures.

Fourth, the ritual transforms the offering from a natural object into something holy and therefore supernatural. Ritual is shrouded in the sanctity that it creates. Its words and gestures are archaic, mysterious, and all the more imperative because they have come down to us unexplained. The voice of ancestors speaks through the ritual, and the one who seeks to change or distort what is done at the altar commits the primary act of sacrilege: he re-creates, and therefore desecrates, the god.

Finally, by a wonderful inversion, which is perhaps the archetype of all miracles, the sacrifice becomes a *sacrament,* something offered *from* the altar to the very person whose gift it is, and which raises him from pollution to purity, from separation to communion, from fall to redemption.

Such a pattern is not observed everywhere, of course.[1] But it lies deep in our own tradition. It can be found throughout the ancient world – in the cults of Demeter and Persephone at Eleusis, for example, and of Diana at Ephesus – and forms the core experience of the Christian Eucharist. And with this pattern of behaviour comes also a pattern of belief. The ceremony is construed as an act of worship, and the thing worshipped is believed to be both distinct from the worshippers and yet united to them by an intense personal concern. The god is a supernatural person, who 'resides' in the shrine where he is worshipped, and who also travels ubiquitously but invisibly in the natural world.

We should distinguish two kinds of religious understanding: the mythical and the theological. Stories of divinities and ghosts, who journey through the world brimful of interest in our doings there, are inseparable from the religious impulse. Unlike the theological doctrines of religion, they give no answer to our mortal questions – no account of the cause or the goal of our existence. They may *suggest* answers; but they are valued and remembered for other reasons. The myth *animates* the world, by

---

1   It is not observed, for example, by Christoph von Fürer-Haimendorf in the Asian hunter-gatherer tribes describe in *Morals and Merit: A Study of Values and Social Controls in South Asian Societies,* London 1967, Chapter 1.

projecting intention and desire into natural processes, by describing nature as a thinking, feeling thing, and thereby lifting the natural to the supernatural. In myth we seem to confront a story which asks to be believed, without being believed as true; a metaphor that we re-enact in the literal language of our own emotions. We find a parallel to the mythic consciousness in art, and many of those (like Jung) who have noticed the parallel have used it to explain the experience of beauty. Myth involves a special kind of thought: a projection of consciousness which also clarifies consciousness, by mingling it with the natural order.

Sacred rites and observances are in a certain sense *meticulous*. Their purpose and power lie in their exact performance. Like magic spells (to which they are closely related) they must be conducted *to the letter*, without error, as custom dictates. Mistakes may be made: but it is important that they be mistakes rather than innovations, since any spontaneous innovation carries a risk of *sacrilege*. The difference between correct observance and sacrilege may be so minute as to be imperceptible to the outsider: the question whether to make the sign of the cross with two fingers or with three once split the Orthodox Church of Russia, with momentous consequences that still affect us.

If we set those facts aside, and consider religious belief simply as a piece of philosophical theology – a speculative answer to the riddle of existence – then it would strike us as extraordinary that there should be reserved, for those who make some small error in their reasoning, the name of heretic, and the terrible punishments which that name invites. In religious belief and observance, however, it is not the large differences that count but the small ones. The nearer someone is to me in his religious convictions, the greater my revulsion at the 'errors' which divide us. The haughty reserve of the Lebanese Shi'ite towards his Christian neighbour in no way compares with his hatred for the Sunni rival, and the distaste with which the Calvinist views the atheist of the modern city seldom matches the vehemence with which he condemns the Catholic Church. Even in the secular religions of our day the fear of heretics has engaged a large part of the church's energies – witness the constant 'struggle' of the communist church against 'deviationism', 'opportunism', 'Trotskyism', 'revisionism' and the rest. Only from a safe distance can any of this be viewed with amusement. For those in the vicinity of real religion, the world presents a stark and disturbing choice between the absolute safety of the orthodox creed, and the mortal danger of denying it from a position within its territory. Heresy and sacrilege are dangerous because they threaten the community: the meticulousness of the religious rite is a sign that religion is not merely a system of belief, but a criterion of membership.

The supernatural realm becomes a reality for us whenever we confront the mystery of death and hover above the abyss. We know then that the riddle of existence cannot be understood in words; that the doctrines of religion, to the extent that they are merely doctrines, must fall far short of an answer. In confronting death we find ourselves facing the vertiginous, the bottomless, the unknowable – the supernatural in its most uncanny form. A primeval horror inhabits all of us – a horror of night and closure and nothingness. The religious rite dispels this horror, uniting us to the community not here and now only, but in the land of the dead.

Anthropologists have noticed the tendency among the people they study to assimilate birth and death to the 'transitions' which signify a change in social status. Funeral rites and birth ceremonies (baptisms) are like the 'rites of passage' that accompany initiation, marriage and the awakening of the tribe from peace to war.[2] All these things are experienced *collectively*, as revelations of the tie of membership. That is how the agony of a death is overcome by those who survive it: death is regarded as a transition to another state *within the community*. The dead person joins the congress of ancestors, and thereby remains in communication with the living. In marking this transition as 'sacred', the tribe is lifting death to the supernatural level, and endowing it – as it endows marriage, birth and war – with divine authority. In the vicinity of death the living are commanded. Moreover, by honouring the dead, recognising obligations towards them, and treating them as part of the community (though a part that has been 'transfigured') a tribe acquires a sense of its identity and duration across generations. The cult of ancestors is the surest motive for sacrifice, and for the 'readiness to die' on which the

---

2   Arnold van Gennep, *Les rites de passage*, Paris 1909.

future of a society depends. It goes hand in hand with caring for offspring, and for offspring's offspring, who come into being as a sacred pledge to those who have departed. The desecration of a grave is, on this account, a primary form of sacrilege, as is any comparable disrespect shown towards the dead. From the sacrilegious treatment of the dead all other impieties stem – and in impious times (such as ours) the disrespect towards ancestors becomes a recurring motif of public life. It is important to bear this in mind when considering the current 'culture wars'.

The funeral rite is a salve for the wound of death because it unites the tribe around its core experience of membership. The dead person does not go from the community, but becomes a permanent, though invisible, part of it. This need not involve a denial of death or a belief in personal immortality: the ritual makes sense at a purely symbolic level, without the benefit of such reflective commentaries. And it shows us the natural origins of the experience of the sacred. Those things are sacred in which the spirit of the community has taken residence, and in which *our* destiny is at stake: as it is at stake, for example, in sexual feelings, in attitudes to children and parents, in the rituals of membership and initiation whereby the first-person plural – the 'we' – is formed. The sexual revolution of modern times has disenchanted the sexual act. Sex has been finally removed from the sacred realm: it has become 'my' affair, in which 'we' no longer show an interest. This de-consecration of the reproductive process is the leading fact of modern culture.

It goes without saying that a common culture binds a society together. But it does so in a special way. The unity of a great society can be achieved by terror, by confronting people with a common danger or an 'enemy within' – by variously playing with the threat of death, in the manner of modern dictators. A common culture is an altogether more peaceful method, which unites the present members by *dedicating* them to the past and future of the community. Death is not a terror, but the benign catalyst of the social order, the transition which ensures that all of us, in time, will join the community of ancestors and become sacred and transfigured as they are.

Since the Enlightenment, it has been normal for Europeans to think of society as a contract. The novelty of the idea is twofold: first, it implies that social membership is a free choice. Second, it suggests that all members of society are currently living. Neither of those thoughts is true. But, without religion, people tend to *believe* that they are true. Even if we recognise the social contract for what it is – a fiction that hides the empty heart of modern politics – we nevertheless find it hard to formulate our social and political obligations in other terms. Burke reacted violently to the social contract as interpreted by the French Revolutionaries. By making the 'people' sovereign, he argued, the Revolution had disenfranchised the dead and the unborn. Care for the dead and care for the unborn go hand-in-hand. Sacrilegious abuse of the dead is also a squandering of social capital. Conversely, by respecting the dead and their wishes we keep intact the accumulated resources of society, and place an obstacle before the living, in their desire to seize all savings for themselves. When a school or foundation is dedicated to the dead, then knowledge and property are rescued from current emergencies, and laid by for future generations. The concept of sacrilege is therefore a safeguarding and conserving force. Without it all resources are open to pillage – a fact of which we, heirs to the Enlightenment, are acutely aware.

Anthropologists study people from an external perspective. They justify practices in terms that would never be used by the people themselves, whose perspective is the internal one of membership. To a visiting anthropologist who observes the rites and customs of a tribe, piety towards the dead has a function: it is justified by the benefit that it confers upon the living. But this benefit is far from the mind of the tribesman. He honours the dead because honour is due to them: his own and others' future has no part in the calculation. Indeed, if he adopted the perspective of the anthropologist, the tribesman would be a threat to the very order that he wishes to protect. For he would be opening the door to doubt, both in himself and in his neighbours. Piety is a means to social unity only when not treated as a means. The function of piety is fulfilled when people do what piety requires, but for no other reason than that piety requires it.

The clash between the internal and external perspectives is a familiar feature of modern experience: Burke's defence of prejudice is one of the first and most vivid instances. For how can you defend prejudice except from the assumption of an open mind? Modern people long for membership; but membership exists only among people who do not long for it, who have no real conception of it, who are so utterly immersed in it that they find it inscribed on the face of nature itself. Such people have immediate access, through common culture, to the ethical vision of man.

The ethical vision is what all religions deliver, and what all societies need – the vision of human beings as objects of judgement. Whether the judge be man or god; whether accounts are settled in this world or the next; whether natural or supernatural powers redeem us, judgement is the core of religion. Looked at from the external point of view this judgement is the imagined voice of the tribe, holding its members to account for the long-term common interest.[3] But from the internal point of view judgement is a *destiny*, from which there is no escape, since no deed can be hidden from supernatural eyes.

The ethical vision endows human matter with a personal form, and therefore lifts us above nature, to set us side by side with our judge. If we are judged then we must be free, and answerable for our actions. The free being is not just an organism: he has a life of his own, which is uniquely his and which he creates through his choices. Hence he stands above nature in the very activities which reveal him to be a part of it. He is not a creature of the moment, but on the contrary a creature extended through time, and compromised forever by his actions. You are answerable now for the deeds of yesterday and accountable tomorrow for the deeds of today. When you stand before the judge it is not your act which is condemned or praised but you yourself, who are the same at the moment of judgement as you were at the moment of action and as you will be for ever more.

This long-term answerability means that the free being is set apart from the natural order. His acts and omissions flow from the inner well-spring of intention. His motives are ranged on the scale of virtue and vice, and he is seen as supernatural beings are seen: subject, not object; cause, not effect; the invisible centre of his world, but in some way not truly a part of it. Kant referred in

---

3   Such, very briefly, is Durkheim's external account of the 'elementary forms of the religious life': see bibliography.

this connection to the 'transcendental self' which is the locus of our freedom. But older idioms strive for the same idea. Soul, spirit, self; the 'I am' of God's word to Moses, the *nafs* (soul, self, individual) of the Koran, and St Paul's metaphor of the face (*prosopon*):

> For now we see through a glass, darkly; but then face to face; now I know in part; but then shall I know even as also I am known. (I Corinthians 13.)

All those idioms are attempts to capture the same vision, of the agent *in* the world who is judged from a point of view outside it – a point of view which is also his own.

The ethical vision of man confers value on the human form, on the human face, the human deed and the human word. It permits the higher emotions, through which we ennoble our lives and the lives of those around us. Erotic and parental love pass through the merely 'empirical' being whom we hold in our arms, and target the elusive and transcendental centre, the god-like nothing which is everything, the light that shines from human eyes but which shines also from an elusive point beyond them. This *revelation of the individual in his freedom* forms one of the primary themes of high art, and it is easy to see why. For it both attracts and forbids description. It causes awe and elation, as though in the presence of a divine mystery. And that is exactly what it is, according to Dante's matchless account in *La vita nuova*.

From the internal point of view, the ethical vision of man is a constant and self-renewing motive to action. It prompts us to accord respect and loyalty to other people. It confers importance, mystery and sanctity on our meanest transactions, and irradiates our actions with a meaningfulness that is not of this world. Hence, from the external point of view, it is a priceless addition to the bond of society. No anthropologist, observing a community in which the tenets of religion have taken root, would wish to disabuse his tribe of their sacred rites and stories. It is only those brought up in the faith who feel the impulse, on losing it, to ruin the faith of others. For the anthropologist, the religion is the mainstay of the culture, and therefore the guarantee of social knowledge.

The ethical vision safeguards social capital; it also releases and assuages social emotions. A common culture permits the deeper feelings, and at the same time educates them. I shall take an example, from Homer's *Odyssey*.

In the hurry to leave Circe's palace, Elpenor, one of Odysseus's band of *hetairoi*, had fallen while drunk to his death. Odysseus and the remaining members of his crew had fled the enchanted isle, leaving Elpenor unburied. When later Odysseus summons the spirits of the dead, it is Elpenor who, in his urgency, is first to appear. He addresses his lord and master thus:

> Now I beseech you, by all those whom you left behind, by your wife and by the father who reared you as a child, and by Telemachus your only son whom you left within your halls, that you will, sailing from the Kingdom of Hades, put in with your good ship at the isle of Aeaea. And there my lord I beseech you to remember me and not to leave me there unwept and unburied, lest I should become a cause of divine wrath against you. But burn me there with all my arms and raise a mound for me by the shore of the grey sea, in memory of an unfortunate man, so that those yet to be will know the place. Do this for me, and on my tomb plant the oar that I used to pull when I was living and rowing beside my companions. (Bk. XI, ll. 66–78.)

It is not simply that Elpenor is asking to be buried; he is asking to be mourned. 'Do not leave me,' he implores, 'unwept and unburied' (*aklauton kai athapton*). Odysseus knows what to do: he must burn Elpenor's body, mourn his passing, and erect a monument. The unborn are crucially involved in this oblation to the dead, and in honouring Elpenor Odysseus acts also for 'those who are yet to be'. His actions are connected, in a way that is immediate to Odysseus's perception, with Odysseus's own love for his family and respect for the father who reared him. The common culture embraces these complex states of mind and reinforces their validity. Elpenor, by demanding grief, confirms all other dutiful feelings. He is confronting Odysseus as one ethical being confronts another – the object of judgement.

No reader of Homer can fail to be impressed by the natural and uncorrupted feeling that flows so abundantly through the characters, making them transparent to each other and also to themselves. In every situation they 'know what to feel', and move unhesitatingly to express and vindicate their view of things. The example of Elpenor casts light on this. The rites and customs of a common culture close the gap between emotion and action: they tell people what to do, precisely in those situations where the ethical vision intrudes – where love, grief, anger or revenge are the proper motives, and where we face each other soul to soul. And because they are socially constructed and socially endorsed, these rites and customs legitimise not only the actions but the feelings that advance through them. It is easier to feel serious emotions, when this is what society expects; easier still when provided with a repertoire of accepted gestures, through which to choreograph and bring order to one's wretchedness. And that is why Elpenor can demand to be mourned: under the benign jurisdiction of a common culture, grief is something you *do*.

The ethical vision of our nature gives sense to our lives. But it is demanding. It asks us to stand up to judgement. We must be fully human, while breathing the air of angels; natural and supernatural at once. A community that has survived its gods has three options. It can find some secular path to the ethical life. Or it can fake the higher emotions, while living without them. Or it can give up pretending, and so collapse, as Burke put it, into the 'dust and powder of individuality'. These are the stark choices that confront us, and the rest of this book defends the first of them – the way of high culture, which teaches us to live *as if* our lives mattered eternally. But first we must go back to Elpenor.

In modern conditions grief is not an easy thing to feel; every person has a reason to avoid it, and may very well try to avoid it, even in the presence of its proper object, which is the death of someone loved. A sort of busying anxiety intervenes to arrest emotion – a haste to clear away the debris, and a numbness which refuses to believe. Emily Dickinson describes the experience in memorable words:

She mentioned, and forgot;
Then lightly as a reed
Bent to the water, struggled scarce,
Consented, and was dead.
And we, we placed the hair

And drew the head erect;
And then an awful leisure was,
Belief to regulate.

In response to death it is important to feel something, and yet there is no precedent, since every death is original, the loss of just *this* individual, just *this* judging gaze. The demand to feel is addressed to me, here, now; it is not detachable from the imperatives of my individual life and present situation. And looking around I find no help, no example, no repertoire on which to draw and with which to elicit the unembarrassed sympathy of my real or imaginary tribe. Deep emotion demands the unseen chorus – the others who will dance with it; when there is no chorus, we flee into solitude and mute refusal. We begin to lose confidence in the vision which makes human life the centre of a cosmic drama. Our emotions then come to us as though from outside, bearing no mark of self, of intention, of commitment or answerability. An 'awful leisure' overcomes us: the leisure of a life that flees from judgement.

There is an important parallel here between common culture and high culture. Since the Enlightenment philosophers have debated the value of high culture (though not necessarily using that term to describe it): what exactly do we *learn* through the study of art, literature, history and music? Are we simply memorising dates and facts, lines and techniques, accumulating a body of literary scholarship? Or is there some other kind of knowledge involved? Here is one answer to those questions:

Knowledge includes three distinct kinds: knowledge *that,* knowledge *how*, and knowledge *what*. I know *that* uranium is radioactive; I know *how* to ride a bicycle; and I sometimes know *what* to do, what to say or what to feel. The first kind of knowledge is information (of which science is the systematic part); the second is skill; the third virtue. In reverse order these correspond to the three inputs into a rational life: the ends, the means and the facts. Knowing what to do, Aristotle suggested, is a matter of right judgement (*orthos logos*); but it also involves *feeling* rightly. The virtuous person 'knows what to feel', and this means feeling what the situation requires: the right emotion, towards the right object, on the right occasion and in the right degree. Moral education has just such knowledge as its goal: it is an education of the emotions. The virtue of the Greek hero is of a piece with his emotional certainty, and this certainty is the gift of culture, and of the higher vision which culture makes available. By setting the individual within the context of the group, by providing him with ritual expressions and the path to collective release, by uniting him in thought with the unborn and the dead, and by imbuing his thoughts with ideas of sanctity and sacrilege, the culture enables the hero to give safe and sincere expression to the feelings that social life requires. The common culture tells him how and what to feel, and in doing so raises his life to the ethical plane, where the thought of judgement inhabits whatever he does.

Something similar has been said of high culture. In studying what Matthew Arnold called 'the best that has been thought and said', we are extending the repertoire of emotion. Lamenting the death of Wordsworth Arnold wrote: 'who, ah who, will make us feel?'[4] As Arnold knew, feeling does not exist in and of itself, in some purely subjective medium, much as we deceive ourselves into thinking the opposite – into believing that we are paragons of sensitivity who are accidentally deprived of the means to reveal it. Feeling exists when it finds objective form, in words, gestures, plans and projects. A feeling involves a picture of the world, and a stance towards it. It is predicated on understanding. The poet, who causes us for a moment to move in time to his emotion and so to re-make it in ourselves, can open the avenues of expression and unfreeze the veins.

The critic Eva Brann said this of Jane Austen's novels:

> They reform the dispersed soul and inculcate respect for the concealed heart. They afford the example of a correct and uncorrupted tongue, and they encourage us to know ourselves and to judge others rightly . . .

True or not, this description says something important about what is imparted to us by novels – not facts or theories but states of mind and moral virtues. Somehow, through reading Austen, Brann suggests, we are restored, much as we are restored through the rites and sacraments of a common religious culture.

---

4   A line rightly criticised by Eliot (*The Use of Poetry and the Use of Criticism*, 2nd Edn., London 1964, p. 107), who nevertheless concurs in Arnold's thought.

There is a making whole, a rejoining of the self to its rightful congregation that come through art and literature. And maybe this is the importance of high culture, that it continues to provide, in a heightened and imaginative form, the ethical vision that religion made so easily available.

If high culture and common culture are connected in such a way, then we can immediately settle that vexatious debate between F.R. Leavis and C.P. Snow, in which the former ridiculed Snow's suggestion that there are now two (high) cultures – the artistic and the scientific – and that, to be truly cultivated, one must be adept in both.[5] On the view that I am proposing, high culture is not a source of scientific or technical knowledge (knowledge *that* or knowledge *how*), but a source of practical wisdom (knowledge *what*). Its meaning lies in the ethical vision that it perpetuates, and in the order that results in our emotions. On such a view, there can no more be a scientific culture than there can be a scientific religion; culture, like religion, addresses the question which science leaves unanswered: the question what to feel. The knowledge that it bestows on us is a knowledge not of facts nor of means but of ends: the most precious knowledge we have.

Many people will find the view that I am advancing preposterous. It seems too far from our post-modern experience, too much a legacy of ways of thinking that are no longer available – or available, if at all, only by studious isolation from the realities of post-modern life. In a certain measure I share this scepticism. Yet I can find no alternative account that explains either the history of high culture or its power. So here are some considerations which might lead us to take the view seriously.

The high culture of Athens centred on the theatre, and in particular on tragedy. But tragedy was a dramatisation and deepening of the religious experience. Tragedies were religious festivals and in many of them we see enacted, in a varied and agonised form, the central drama of the cult – the drama of the

---

5   C.P. Snow, *The Two Cultures and the Scientific Revolution*, Cambridge 1960, and F.R. Leavis, 'Two Cultures? the Significance of Lord Snow', in F.R. Leavis, *Nor Shall my Sword: Discourses on Pluralism, Compassion and Social Hope*, London 1972.

individual, who falls from grace by some sacred fault, and is thereby sundered from his congregation. The *catharsis* (as Aristotle described it) that is brought about by the hero's death is itself a religious feeling – a sense of the restored community, into which, through death and transfiguration, the erring hero is reabsorbed. The movement of many Greek tragedies can best be understood in terms of the religious archetype of the cult – for this makes sense of the strange experience of peace that emerges from these obligatory murders.

In no genuinely religious epoch is the high culture separate from the religious rite. Religious art, religious music and religious literature form the central strand of high culture in all societies where a common religious culture holds sway. Moreover, when art and religion begin to diverge – as they have done in Europe since the Renaissance – it is usually because religion is in turmoil or declining. When art and religion are healthy, they are also inseparable.

Finally, if you consider the high culture of modern times, you will be struck by the theme of alienation which runs through so many of its products. Modern literature, art and music speak of the isolated individual, his quest for home and community or his lapse into solitude and estrangement. It is as though the high culture of our society, having ceased to be a meditation on the common religion, has become instead a meditation on the lack of it. And some of the greatest works of art of our epoch are attempts – like the *Four Quartets* of T.S. Eliot, the *Duino Elegies* of Rilke, or Proust's *Remembrance of Things Past* – to discover an inward and imagined restoration of the self, that would have the redeeming force of cult, community and sacrament.

True, those observations are anecdotal. But they suggest that the connections between common culture and high culture are deep, and that the two cultures perhaps stem from the same psychic need – the need for an ethical community into which the self can be absorbed, its transgressions overcome and forgiven, and its emotions re-made in uncorrupted form. The community offered by art is only imagined, born from the currents of sympathy that animate the realm of fictions. But consolation from imaginary things is not an imaginary consolation.

The connection is further confirmed by reflecting on the sacred text and its meaning. Writing transforms religion as it transforms everything. The universal religions are precisely those whose deities reside not in idols or temples but in texts, and the God of Israel makes explicit in the second commandment that, being defined by a text (the tables of the law), he can tolerate no 'graven images'. The text has the universality of thought: it emancipates itself from place and time and addresses itself to all who can read or hear. Although the local shrine may retain its holiness, it is holy, nevertheless, only as an *instance* of the god's visitations. Other places, equally holy, are admitted as 'consecrated' ground. The prime source of sanctity now becomes the universal ritual, which may be conducted in any consecrated place. It is times rather than places which attract the greatest aura of sanctity – the hours of worship, as in the Muslim faith, the holy days and days of obligation of the Christians and the Jews. The rite becomes imbued with thought; its words become sacred, not to be altered unless by some great authority empowered to speak for the god himself. Hence, virtually all serious liturgies are phrased in some antique language or historic idiom. They must remain unchanged in the midst of change, like the voice of God. That is how a cult becomes a church, and membership emancipates itself from kinship, tribe and locality to become a 'communion of the faithful'.

Although the purpose of an act of worship lies beyond the moment, in the form of a promised redemption from the original sin of solitude, it cannot really be separated from the liturgical means. Means and end are inextricable. Thought and experience are inseparable in the liturgy, as they are in art. Changes in the liturgy are of great significance to the believer, since they are changes in the experience of God. The question whether or not to use the Book of Common Prayer or the Tridentine Mass are not questions of 'mere form'. To suppose that the rite is a matter of form is to imagine just the kind of separation of form and content which is the death (the death by protestation) of a true common culture.

Enlightened people often mock the controversies surrounding the liturgy, and profess not to understand the desire for the old words, save for 'aesthetic reasons'. They are right to see a resemblance between aesthetic interest and the act of worship. But they are wrong in thinking this resemblance to be merely accidental. The quasi-aesthetic absorption in the holy words and gestures is a component in the redemptive process. In participating, the believer is effecting a change in his spiritual standing. The ceremony is not so much a means to this end as a prefiguration of it. In the ritual the believer *confronts* God, and is purified by standing in God's gaze.

The jealousy over the liturgy is of a piece with God's jealousy over idols. Sacred words do not issue from the merely human voice, but from the deity: like the Koran or the Bible, they are dictated from the transcendental realm. When a text is eternal, unalterable, and an expression of God's changeless will, there arises a need for commentary. As time goes on, the application of these holy words becomes ever more obscure, ever more bound in contradiction, ever more polluted by circumstance. Their very venerable character, which places them beyond question, surrounds them with questions. Hence the art of interpretation – hermeneutics – is an essential part of any culture founded on sacred texts. The people stand increasingly in need of the mediator who will elucidate God's word, without detracting from its absolute authority.

Where texts are sacred, the written word becomes the primary vehicle of communication, the paradigm way of giving permanent and meaningful expression to experience. Other texts too obtain an aura of sanctity, and are studied for their deeper meanings. This attitude to the written word again illustrates the continuity between high culture and a religious tradition, and suggests that the first is built upon the second.

We find a telling illustration of this in the predicament of literary studies. If students are to read and analyse literary texts, then surely there ought to be some agreement as to *which* texts are to be studied? If *any* text will do, then so will no text. Only if the texts are in some way self-selecting can an education be constructed from the art of reading them. Hence the need for a 'canon' or tradition of literature, in which the store of literary knowledge is sequestered and from which it can be gleaned. But when young people are brought up without a sacred text, they find it difficult to understand that the secret of life could be obtained in anything so inanimate as a *book* – especially not a book written thousands of years ago in a language which is no longer spoken. Professors find themselves in a quandary, when it comes to explaining why their students should be reading George Eliot rather than Irvine Welsh, or why they should be reading at all, rather than watching MTV. It is pointless to run through the weighty arguments of Leavis, to show that George Eliot is central to the Great Tradition. For in the nature of things, the arguments of a critic are addressed only to those who already have sufficient reverence for literature; for only they will see the point of detailed study and moral interrogation.

This quandary underlies many of the battles over the curriculum in our time. We will understand those battles, it seems to me, only if we recognise the connection between high culture and religion, and the pathos of high culture, when finally severed from the experience of sacred things.

But here we must pause. The idea of the sacred, and the common culture that nurtures it, are no longer easily available. Nor have they enjoyed, since the Enlightenment, their previous dominance in human affairs. At the same time, it is precisely since the Enlightenment that theories of culture have arisen. It is as though culture were noticed for the first time, at the very moment when the older forms of it were vanishing. We should do well, therefore, to gain an overview of the Enlightenment, one legacy of which is the subject-matter of this book.

3
Enlightenment

The Enlightenment began with the rise of modern science, culminated in the French Revolution and then dwindled in wave after wave of yearning, hope and doubt. It was characterised by a scepticism towards authority, a respect for reason, and an advocacy of individual freedom rather than divine command as the basis of moral and political order. The Enlightenment expressed itself in many ways, according to national character and local conditions; but it owes its most celebrated definition to Kant who, in 1784, described it as 'the liberation of man from his self-imposed minority', adding that this minority lies 'not in lack of understanding, but in a lack of determination and courage to use it without the assistance of another'.[1] By the time of Kant's words the Enlightenment was at its crisis. Herder's advocacy of 'culture' against 'civilisation' was in part a reaction to Kant's view of human nature, as formed from a single pattern and fulfilled in a single way – through reason, freedom and law. The 'universalism' advocated by Kant seemed to Herder to threaten all that is most precious in the human soul – namely, the local, the loyal and the rooted.

It would be absurd to suppose that the Enlightenment is one phenomenon, or that it can be defined in any way less vague than Kant's. But it is worth identifying some of the intellectual, emotional and political transformations that occurred in the wake of the scientific revolution, since they affected all that came thereafter, and have left their indelible mark on modern culture.

First there is the transformation noticed by Herder. Enlightened people cease to define themselves in terms of place, history, tribe or dynasty, and lay claim instead to a universal

---

1   Immanuel Kant, 'An Answer to the Question: "What is Enlightenment?"': see bibliography.

human nature, whose laws are valid for all mankind. For Kant, tribal, racial and dynastic loyalties were to give way to a universal jurisdiction, which would guarantee peace by eroding the local jealousies that threaten it.

Then comes the retreat of the sacred. The gods and saints cease to haunt their shrines, the old ceremonies lose their divine authority, the sacred texts are put in question, and doubt is cast on all but the most abstract versions of religious doctrine. This process had begun with the Reformation and Luther's 'priesthood of all believers'. But it took a peculiar turn during the eighteenth century, as people began to look on the sacred texts and stories as metaphors rather than literal truths. The abstract deism of Voltaire and Kant sees religion as an unmediated relation between God and self. Knowledge of God comes through our own reasoning powers and through the exercise of moral choice, without the aid of images, texts or rituals.[2] So defined, the line between deism and atheism is a fine one.

By the same token, inherited authority loses its grip. For the Enlightenment, nobody has a 'divine right' to obedience. All authority rests in the free choice of those who submit to it. No government is legitimate, therefore, until freely accepted by its subjects. Political organisation is envisaged as a 'social contract' between freely choosing individuals, rather than an inherited tie.

With the retreat of the gods and the loss of roots Enlightenment thinkers found themselves launched on a new quest – not for the divine, but for the natural. Rousseau's 'noble savage' has haunted Western literature ever since he stepped from his creator's doubt-tormented brain. Man, in Rousseau's account, has been corrupted by society. To rediscover our freedom we must measure every activity against its 'natural' counterpart. Not that we can return to our 'natural' state; the very idea of a state of nature is a philosophical abstraction. Nevertheless, in everything there is *another way*, an as yet undiscovered route to authenticity, which will allow us to do freely what we now do only by constraint. No existing institution should be accepted, therefore, just because it is existing. Every practice and custom should be

---

2 I am simplifying, of course. The full and noble picture is given by Kant himself, in *Religion within the Limits of Reason Alone*.

questioned, measured against an *a priori* standard, and amended if it fails to come up to the mark.

Such ideas altered the cultural climate of Europe and America. The Enlightenment thereafter became a central preoccupation of sociology. Ferdinand Tönnies, for example, formulated a distinction between two kinds of society – *Gemeinschaft* and *Gesellschaft* – the first based in affection, kinship and historic attachment, the second in division of labour, self-interest and free association by contract and exchange.[3] Traditional societies, he argued, are of the first kind, and construe obligations and loyalties in terms of a non-negotiable destiny. Modern societies are of the second kind, and therefore regard all institutions and practices as provisional, to be revised in the light of our changing requirements. The transition from *Gemeinschaft* to *Gesellschaft* is part of what happened at the Enlightenment, and one explanation for the vast cultural changes, as people learned to view their obligations in contractual terms, and so envisage a way to escape them.

Max Weber wrote, in the same connection, of a transition from traditional to 'legal-rational' forms of authority, the first sanctioned by immemorial usage, the second by impartial law.[4] To these two distinctions can be added yet another, due to Sir Henry Maine, who described the transition from traditional to modern societies as a shift from status to contract – i.e. a shift from inherited social position, to a position conferred by, and earned through, consent.[5]

Those sociological ideas are attempts to understand changes whose effect has been so profound that we have not yet come to terms with them. Still less had people come to terms with them in the late eighteenth century, when the French Revolution sent shock waves through the elites of Europe. The social contract seemed to lead of its own accord to a tyranny far darker than any monarchical excess: the contract between each of us became an enslavement of all. Enlightenment and the fear of Enlightenment were henceforth inseparable. Burke's attack on the Revolution

---

3   Ferdinand Tönnies, *Gemeinschaft und Gesellschaft,* 1887.

4   Max Weber, *Wirtschaft und Gesellschaft,* Tübingen, 1922.

5   Sir Henry Maine, *Ancient Law,* Oxford, 1861.

illustrates this new state of mind. His argument is a sustained defence of 'prejudice' – by which he meant the inherited store of human wisdom, whose value lasts only so long as we do not question it – against the 'reason' of Enlightenment thinking. But people have prejudices only when they see no need to defend them. Only an enlightened person could think as Burke did, and the paradox of his position is now a familiar sub-text of modern culture – the sub-text of conservatism.

Burke's 'prejudice' corresponds more or less exactly to Herder's 'culture'. Both writers are attempting to define and endorse in retrospect the kind of social order that I described in the previous chapter – the order of sacred things. People bound by a common culture see the world as visited by benign and spiritual powers, who establish rights of territory and historic ties. In the wake of the French Revolution, and in reaction against it, nationalist movements attempted to revive these historic ties, but without their religious basis. The Nation assumed the authority that had been torn from the heads of kings, and the result was a new and dangerous form of idolatry. We should not blame Burke or Herder for this; they were merely lamenting what they foresaw, should the Enlightenment finally triumph over inherited attachments. And for the twentieth-century historian it is hard to tell which has been most destructive – the 'particularist' creeds of nationalist demagogues like Fichte, or the 'universalist' ideas of their revolutionary opponents, such as Marx.

It was Marx who developed the most popular explanation of the Enlightenment. The Enlightenment saw itself as the triumph of reason over superstition. But the real triumph, Marx argued, lay not in the sphere of ideas but in the sphere of economics. The aristocratic order had been destroyed, and with it the feudal relations which bound the producers to the land and the consumers to the court. In place of the old order came the 'bourgeois' economy, based on the wage contract, the division of labour and private capital. The contractual view of society, the emphasis on individual freedom, the belief in impartial law, the attack on superstition in the name of reason – all these cultural phenomena are part of the 'ideology' of the new bourgeois order, contributions to the self-image whereby the capitalist class ratifies its usurpation.

The Marxist theory is a form of economic determinism, distinguished by the belief that fundamental changes in economic relations are invariably revolutionary, involving a violent overthrow of the old order, and a collapse of the political 'superstructure' which had been built on it. The theory is almost certainly false: nevertheless, there is something about the Marxian picture which elicits, in enlightened people, the will to believe. By explaining culture as a by-product of material forces, Marx endorses the Enlightenment view, that material forces are the only forces there are. The old culture, with its gods and traditions and authorities, is made to seem like a web of illusions – 'the opiate of the people', which quietens their distress.

Hence, in the wake of the Enlightenment, there came not only the reaction typified by Burke and Herder, and embellished by the romantics, but also a countervailing cynicism towards the very idea of culture. It became normal to view culture from outside, not as a mode of thought which defines our moral inheritance, but as an elaborate disguise, through which artificial powers represent themselves as natural rights. Thanks to Marx, debunking theories of culture have become a part of culture. And these theories have the structure pioneered by Marx: they identify power as the reality, and culture as the mask; they also foretell some future 'liberation' from the lies that have been spun by our oppressors.

Debunking theories of culture are popular for two reasons: because they are linked to a political agenda, and because they provide us with an overview. If we are to understand the Enlightenment, then we need such an overview. But ought it to be couched in these external terms? After all, the Enlightenment is part of us; people who have not responded to its appeal are only half awake to their condition. It is not enough to *explain* the Enlightenment; we must also *understand* it.

The distinction between explanation and understanding itself came to us from the Enlightenment. Vico hinted at it in his theory of history, as did Kant in his moral philosophy. Inspired by Kant's account of practical reason, the romantic theologian Friedrich Schleiermacher argued that the interpretation of human actions can never be accomplished by the methods employed by the natural sciences. The human act must be understood as the act of a free subject, motivated by reason. The same is true of texts, which can be interpreted, thought Schleiermacher, only through an imaginative dialogue with their authors. Hermeneutics – the art of interpretation – involves the search for reasons rather than causes. We understand texts as expressions of rational activity, the very activity that is manifest in us as we interpret them.

A later Kantian philosopher, Wilhelm Dilthey, extended Schleiermacher's hermeneutical 'method' to the entire human world. We seek to understand human actions, he argued, not by explaining them in terms of external causes, but 'from within', by an act of rational self-projection that Dilthey called *Verstehen*. In understanding human life and action, we look for the concepts which inspire and guide it. Thus I understand your fear of speaking in a certain place, once I conceptualise it as you do, as somewhere 'sacred'. This is not an act of scientific explanation, but an act of human sympathy, the outcome of an implied or actual dialogue.

It is not only individual human beings who are the objects of *Verstehen*. Understanding can be directed towards the entire human world – the world of institutions, customs, laws and culture. *Verstehen* is cultivated through those studies which look for reasons, meanings, and values, rather than causes: through the humanities rather than the natural sciences. And the end result is, or ought to be, an internal perspective on the life, thought and motivation of our fellow human beings, rather than a science of their behaviour. The human world is a world of significances, and no human significance can be fully grasped by science. Every expression must be returned to its social, historical and cultural context if its full meaning is to be revealed; hence *Verstehen* must be educated through comparison and critical analysis.

Those ideas are controversial, but they contain at least one indisputable truth, and one to which I have already drawn attention. Upon every culture there is an internal and an external perspective – the perspective of the tribesman and that of the anthropologist. Homer's *Odyssey* enables us to share the internal perspective on an enchanted world. Thanks to such artists as Pope, Goethe and Mozart, we can acquire the same internal perspective on the sober world of the Enlightenment. They show us what it was like, to live through the loss of old authority, and to see the vision unfold of man in his freedom, with his dignity not yet degraded, and his religion not yet crumbled to dust. In art, literature and music, the Enlightenment gave content to its universalism, with stories, epics and operas that might be set in any place or time, each devoted to the human substance beneath the local colour. Its criticisms of old authority were accompanied by a fervent and pious attempt to retain the ethical view of man. In the very act of re-casting marriage as a contract and authority as a myth, the Enlightenment showed how men and women can re-dignify these things which have lost their sanctity, and make of them a lasting monument to human hopes. Such is the message of the *Henriade* and the *Lettres Persanes,* of *Wilhelm Meister* and *The Magic Flute,* and through such works we see that the Enlightenment was not the single and simple thing described by Marx. Nor was it merely a transitional period, with a before and after that are clearly distinct from it. The Enlightenment, we discover, is part of us. It belongs to the archaeology, rather than the pre-history, of modern consciousness.

But, as I noted in discussing Burke, Enlightenment goes hand in hand with the fear of it. From the very beginning hope and doubt have been intertwined. What if men needed those old authorities, needed the habit of obedience and the sense of the sacred? What if, without them, they should jettison all loyalties, and give themselves to a life of godless pleasure? In a penetrating view from within of the Enlightenment mentality – a view made possible by Mozart – Nicholas Till has shown us how real were these fears.[6] Furthermore, the very aim for a universal culture, without time or place, brought a new kind of loneliness. Communities depend upon the force which Burke called prejudice; they are essentially local, bound to a place, a history, a language and a common culture. The Enlightened individualist, by forgoing such things, lives increasingly as a stranger among strangers, consumed by a helpless longing for an attachment which his own cold thinking has destroyed.

These conflicts within Enlightenment culture are part of its

---

6   Nicholas Till, *Mozart and the Enlightenment,* London 1992.

legacy to us. We too are individualists, believers in the sovereign right of human freedom, living as strangers in a society of strangers. And we too are beset by those ancient and ineradicable yearnings for something else – for a homecoming to our true community. The theme of homecoming is at the root of German romanticism, finds its highest expression in the poetry of Hölderlin, and dominates political thinking in the German tradition – both the revolutionary evangelism of Marx, with its promise of a 'full communism' in which man will be 'restored to himself', and the reactionary nationalism of Fichte and Gierke, for whom the *Volk* and the *Volksgeist* were the primary objects of social hope. But if there is anything to be learned from the movements which those thinkers created, it is that there is no going back, that we must live with our enlightened condition and endure the inner tension to which it condemns us. And it is in terms of this tension, I believe, that we should understand both the splendours and the miseries of modern culture.

4
The Aesthetic Gaze

It is normal to relate the decline of Christian faith to the Enlightenment. It is not quite so normal to relate the rise of aesthetics to the decline of faith. Nevertheless, as faith became more spectral, beauty took on flesh. The Romantic movement in art and literature, the cult of natural beauty and the picturesque, and the rise of philosophical aesthetics all indicate a fundamental shift in attitude.

Marxists have gone further, dating not merely the *concept* of the aesthetic to the Enlightenment, but the thing itself. This claim, however, is implausible. The *word* 'aesthetic' was given its modern use in the eighteenth century (by A.G. Baumgarten, a German disciple of Leibniz); but the phenomena which he used it to describe are as old as history, and the problems of aesthetics are discussed (in other terms) by Plato and Aristotle.

Still, something significant happened, shortly after 1750, when Baumgarten published his *Aesthetica*. Art, music, poetry and natural beauty began to take on the momentous importance in intellectual life that they have retained to this day. The aesthetic began to replace the religious as the central strand in education. Art and literature ceased to be recreations, and became *studies,* devoted, as divinity had been devoted, to the nurturing and refining of the soul.[1]

Kant, who wrote the first great modern work of philosophical aesthetics – the *Critique of Judgement* – went further. He did not merely shift the focus from theology to aesthetics: he

---

1   Although the chronology of such things cannot be precisely defined, it is significant that in 1751 Adam Smith was already including *Belles Lettres* in his lectures as Glasgow Professor of Logic, and that by 1762 a Regius Chair of Rhetoric and *Belles Lettres* had been founded in Edinburgh, with Hugh Blair as tenant.

actually derived his theology from his aesthetics, using aesthetic judgement as the proof of God. It is through aesthetic contemplation, he suggested, that we confront the aspect of the world which was the traditional concern of theology. We cannot prove by theoretical reasoning that there is a God; nor can we grasp the *idea* of God, except by a *via negativa* that forbids us to apply it. Nevertheless, we have intimations of the transcendental. In the sentiment of beauty we feel the purposiveness and intelligibility of everything that surrounds us, while in the sentiment of the sublime we seem to see beyond the world, to something overwhelming and inexpressible in which it is somehow grounded. Neither sentiment can be translated into a reasoned argument – for such an argument would be natural theology, and natural theology is a thing of the past, believable only in an age of unquestioning faith. All we know is that we can know nothing of the transcendental. But that is not what we *feel* – and it is in our feeling for beauty that the content, and even the truth, of religious doctrine is strangely and untranslatably intimated to us.

We might put the point thus: knowledge of God is not a knowledge *that,* nor a knowledge *how,* but a knowledge *what*: a knowledge what to feel in the face of nature. That is not Kant's way of putting it but mine; but it again takes us back to the heart of common culture, and the underlying experience to which even Kant's supremely enlightened philosophy obliquely points – the experience of the tribe.

The *Critique of Judgement* situates the aesthetic experience and the religious experience side by side, and tells us that it is the first, and not the second, which is the archetype of revelation. It is aesthetic experience which reveals the *sense* of the world. Of course, the 'sense' turns out to be, for Kant, precisely what religion had assumed it to be. But suppose we do not accept that conclusion? Suppose we look for the meaning of the world in aesthetic experience, while reserving judgement in matters of faith? This would be to give to aesthetic interest an importance comparable to that which once attached to religious worship. And surely, this elevation of the aesthetic to the highest spiritual position is exactly what we find, not only in Kant, but in the long tradition of philosophers, critics and poets which followed in the wake of German romanticism, and which led, in our time, to the invention of English as an academic discipline, and to the modernist movement in the arts.

But what exactly does the word 'aesthetic' mean? The question is not just one of definition – it is one of discovery, identification and description. There is a state of mind, an attitude, a stance towards the world, for which we have borrowed, under the influence of Enlightenment philosophers, a Greek word that means something quite different. (*Aesthesis* denotes sensation or perception.) Why have we singled out this state of mind (if that is what it is)? What is important about it, and why should it have been ennobled by so many artists and thinkers, to sit on a throne archaically devoted to the gods?

Those questions are among the most difficult that philosophers have to confront – which perhaps explains why no philosophers now confront them. You cannot expect an impregnable theory of the aesthetic in two pages. Nevertheless, we need a theory of *some* kind, and what follows is the best I can do.

Rational activity involves both ends and means. In a technological age we acquire an increasing grasp of the means to our goals, and a decreasing grasp of the reasons why we should pursue them. The clarity of purpose that I observed in Homer's Odysseus is not a clarity about means: it is a clarity about ends, about the things that are worth doing *for their own sake*, like grieving and loving and honouring the gods. The mastery of means that emancipated mankind from drudgery has brought with it a mystery of ends – an inability to answer, to one's own satisfaction, the question what to feel or do. The mystery deepens with the advent of the consumer society, when all the channels of social life are devoted to consumption. For consumption, in its everyday form, is not really an *end*. It destroys the thing consumed and leaves us empty-handed: the consumer's goals are perpetually recurring illusions, which vanish at the very moment they loom into view, destroyed by the appetite that seeks them. The consumer society is therefore phantasmagoric, a place in which the ghosts of satisfactions are pursued by the ghosts of real desires.[2]

---

2   That which is, to my mind, most enduring in Marx's contribution to the study of political economy, is his recognition of the hallucinogenic character of a money-economy, as exemplified by what

In the world of religion all things appear in two guises: as instruments for our uses, and as creations, earthly manifestations of some higher design. The myths and sacred stories shine through their earthly instances, and the ordinary world is transfigured into a realm of miracles. Everything is what it is, while representing something else – the higher form of itself that is narrated in the myth. The world of Odysseus has not been 'instrumentalised'; it has not yet been enslaved by the imperatives of human desire. Still less is it a world of consumables, to be devoured by relentless and ultimately purposeless appetites. Objects in this world are both instruments and signs: and, in their semantic aspect, they reflect back to the observer a vision of his social life. He confronts in them not objects only, but the eyes of the gods, who remind him of his duties and offer comforting, socially endorsed instructions. In modern jargon, the Greek hero is not *alienated* from the things he uses, but lives with them on terms of respect, finding in the midst of means, the ends which make them useful.

Take away religion, however, and this easy path to comfort is at once overgrown with doubt and fear and selfishness. Add technological mastery, and nature begins to lose all trace of the divine; the old mysteries and myths give way to the new mystery – the mystery of ends in a world of means. In such a predicament people experience a deep-down need for the thing that is not just desired but valued: the *unconsumable* thing, wanted not as a means but for its own sake, as an end. The idea of the sacred satisfies that need – but only by requiring faith and devotion. Besides, it is not the sacred object which is the end but the god who shines through it. The peculiarity of the sacred object is that it is a *necessary* means, one that cannot be replaced or discarded, without fundamentally changing the character of the god to which it is the avenue. Hence sacred objects are filled with an aura of meaning – they are places where calculation stops, where the endless pursuit of means is measured against a value which is not instrumental but intrinsic.

Imagine a sacred statue of the god, placed within its shrine, visited by worshippers who lay their gifts before it. Among the

he called 'commodity fetishism'; see *Capital,* vol. 1, ch. 1, section 4.

visitors is an enlightened philosopher. He does not worship, since he no longer believes in the god; but he is moved by the reverential atmosphere, by the sublime stillness of the sculpture, and the serene belief to which it testifies. He does not address the image with religious feeling as his neighbours do; he does not treat it as an avenue through which another and higher being can be approached and mollified. His emotion attaches to the image itself. The signifier has become the signified. It is *this* thing, the statue, which is or contains the meaning of the shrine. The enlightened visitor directs his attention to the stone, to the way it is worked and finished, to the expression on the face of the god, and the breathing limbs of marble. It is an image of the divine, replete with a more than human tenderness and concern. These epithets describe not the god but the statue. The enlightened visitor does not believe the sacred story; so far as he is concerned, the god is a fiction. His awe is not religious, but aesthetic. To put it another way: he rejoices in the statue, not for the god's sake, but for its own sake. Every meaning that he finds in this marble figure resides, for him, in the figure itself. To the believer the statue is a means to the god; to the philosopher the god is a means to the statue. Yet neither is guilty of idolatry.

I have described there a paradigm case of aesthetic interest. The visitor is interested in the sculpture not as an instrument or a document, but for its own sake. The interest is essentially visual, and bound up with the appearance of what is seen. Aesthetic interest is not cut off from intellectual or spiritual concerns: for these too affect the experience. The god's face has a serene appearance, and this serenity, which invades the face and shines from it, is part of the way the statue looks. In aesthetic interest appearances become signs – signs of themselves.

Kant described aesthetic interest as 'disinterested'. This is what I take him to mean:

All animals have interests. They are interested in satisfying their needs and desires, and in gathering the information required for their well-being. Rational beings have such interests, and use their reason in pursuing them. But they also have 'interests of reason': interests which arise from their rationality, and which are in no clear way related to desires, needs and appetites. One of these, according to Kant, is morality. Reason motivates us to do our duty, and all other ('empirical') interests are discounted in the process. That is what it *means* for a decision to be a moral one. The interest in doing right is not an interest of mine, but an interest of reason *in* me.

Reason also has an interest in the sensuous world. When a cow stands in a field ruminating, and turning her eyes to view the horizon, we can say that she is interested in what is going on (and in particular, in the presence of potential threats to her safety), but not that she is interested in the *view*. A rational being, by contrast, takes pleasure in the mere sight of something: a sublime landscape, a beautiful animal, an intricate flower, or a work of art. This form of pleasure answers to no empirical interest: I satisfy no bodily appetite or need in contemplating the landscape, nor do I merely scan it for useful information. The interest is disinterested – an interest in the landscape for its own sake, for the very thing that it is (or rather, for the very thing that it appears). Disinterestedness is a mark of an 'interest of reason'. We cannot refer it to our empirical nature, but only to the reason that transcends empirical nature, and which searches the world for a meaning that is more authoritative and more complete than any that flows from desire.

On this account, we should hardly be surprised to discover that the aesthetic is a realm of *value*. We perceive in the objects of aesthetic interest a meaning beyond the moment – a meaning which also *resides* in the moment, incarnate, as it were, in a sensory impression. The disinterested observer is haunted by a question: is it right to take pleasure in *this*? Hence arises the idea of taste. We discriminate between the objects of aesthetic interest, find reasons for and against them, and see in each other's choice the sign and expression of moral character. A person who needs urgently to cut a rope and therefore takes up the knife that lies beside him, does not, in choosing that instrument, reveal his character. The knife is a means, and it was the best means to hand. The person with no such use for the knife, who nevertheless places it on his desk and endlessly studies it, thereby shows something of himself. Aesthetic interest does not stem from our passing desires: it reveals what we are and what we value. Taste, like style, is the man himself.

The same is true of all experiences and activities in which

something is treated not as a means, but as an end in itself. When I work, my activity is generally a means to an end – making money, for example. When I play, however, my activity is an end in itself. Play is not a means to enjoyment; it is the very thing enjoyed. And it provides the archetype of other activities that penetrate and give sense to our adult lives: sport, conversation, socialising, and all that we understand by art. Schiller noticed this, and went so far as to exalt play into the paradigm of intrinsic value. With the useful and the good, he remarked, man is merely in earnest; but with the beautiful he *plays. (Letters on the Aesthetic Education of Man.)*

There is an element of paradoxism in Schiller's remark. But you can extract from it a thought that is far from paradoxical, namely this: if every activity is a means to an end, then no activity has intrinsic value. The world is then deprived of its sense. If, however, there are activities that we engage in for their own sake, the world is restored to us and we to it. For of these activities we do not ask what they are *for;* they are sufficient in themselves. Play is one of them; and its association with childhood reminds us of the essential innocence and exhilaration that attends such 'disinterested' activities. If work becomes play – so that the worker is fulfilled in his work, regardless of what results from it – then work ceases to be drudgery, and becomes instead 'the restoration of man to himself'. Those last words are Marx's, and contain the core of his theory of 'unalienated labour' – a theory which derives from Kant, via Schiller and Hegel.

Consider conversation: each utterance calls forth a rejoinder; but in the normal case there is no direction towards which the conversation tends. The participants respond to what they hear with matching remarks, but the conversation proceeds unpredictably and purposelessly, until business interrupts it. Although we gain much information from conversation, this is not its primary purpose. In the normal case, as when people 'pass the time of day', conversation is engaged in for its own sake, like play. The same is true of dancing.

These paradigms of the purposeless can be understood only if we take care to distinguish purpose from function. A socio-biologist will insist that play has a function: it is the safest way to explore the world, and to prepare the child for action. But function is not purpose. The child plays in order to play: play is its own purpose. If you make the function into the purpose – playing for the sake of learning, say – then you cease to play. You are now, as Schiller puts it, 'merely in earnest'. Likewise the urgent person, who converses in order to gain or impart some information, to elicit sympathy or to tell his story, has ceased to converse. Like the Ancient Mariner, he is the death of dialogue.

The same is true of friendship. This too has a function. It binds people together, makes communities strong and durable, brings advantages to those who are joined by it and fortifies them in their endeavours. But make these advantages into your purpose, and the friendship is gone. Friendship is a means to advantage, but only when not treated as a means. The same applies to almost everything worthwhile: education, sport, hiking, fishing, hunting, and art. If we are to live properly, therefore – not merely consuming the world but loving it and valuing it – we must cultivate the art of finding ends where we might have found only means. We must learn when and how to set our interests aside, not out of boredom or disgust, but out of disinterested passion for the thing itself.

Of the greatest importance in our lives, therefore, are festive occasions, when we join with other people in doing purposeless things. Sport – and spectator sport in particular – provides a telling instance of this. Look back to the first flowering of our civilisation in ancient Greece, and you will find sport already in the centre of social life, a focus of loyalties, a rehearsal of military prowess and a pious tribute to the gods. Pindar wrote in praise of winners at the pan-Hellenic games. But his odes are not records of the fleeting victories of the various contestants. They are descriptions of the gods and their stories, invocations of the divine presence in a place and a time, and an exalted celebration of what it means to be a Hellene among Hellenes, sharing language, history, divinities and fate. They show us the spectator as another participant. His excited cheers, we recognise, are brought up from the very depths of his social being, as a contribution to the action and a kind of recreation of the religious sense. Where there is a true common culture, sport is always a central part of it; and the joyful abundance of religious feeling floods over the event: the gods too are present in the hippodrome, eagerly encouraging their favourites.

A modern football match differs from the ancient chariot race in many ways, the most important being the lack of a religious focus. Nevertheless there are important analogies, most readily observable in the American case, with its great hulks fighting each other like armoured knights for every inch of the field, its roaring crowds in their Sabbath humour, its cheer-leaders bouncing and bobbing with choreographed movements and girlish shouts, its jazz groups and marching bands in uniform, its swirling banners and hand-held vacillating flags. In such events we see a kind of collective exultation which is also an exaltation of the community of fans. There is, here, a near return to that experience of membership which I described in Chapter 2, and even if the gods do not take part, you sense them rising in their graves, to peer with shy fascination from behind the screen of our forgetting.

The interest in sport is not yet an aesthetic interest: for there is the unpredictable outcome, the partisanship, the triumph and disaster, towards which all the action is subservient. But it is proximate to the aesthetic, just as it is proximate to the religious. The shared and festive exultation lifts the event high above the world of means, and endows it with a meaning. The game has some of the representational quality of the aesthetic object. It both is itself and stands for itself; once played it becomes a mythic narrative in the annals of the sport, and a tale of heroes. The surplus of interest in the world which spills over in sport is the mark of rational beings, who are satisfied only by supremely useless things.

Still, there is something transient and unfulfilling in even the most exciting football match: the narrative of the match, the myth, can be repeated; but the match, once played, is gone. In aesthetic contemplation, however, we finally step out of the world of perishable things, and find the *unconsumable object,* which is a value in itself. Such things offer visions of the end of life, emancipated from the means. Some of these objects – landscapes, seascapes and skies – are found. But others are made – and when we make them we are consciously addressing what is most attentive, most searching and most responsive in our nature. When the aesthetic becomes a human goal, therefore, it situates itself of its own accord at the apex of our communicative efforts. We make objects replete with meaning, which present human life in its permanent aspect, through fictions and images that enable us to set aside our interests and take stock of the world.

That brief account of aesthetic interest enables us to cast light on high culture. A high culture is a tradition, in which objects made for aesthetic contemplation renew through their allusive power the experience of membership. Religion may wither and festivals decline without destroying high culture, which creates its own 'imagined community', and which offers, through the aesthetic experience, a 'rite of passage' into the kingdom of ends.[3]

Aesthetic objects, when made, invite us to an 'interest of reason' – a self-conscious placing of ourselves in relation to the thing considered, and a search for meaning which looks neither for information nor practical utility, but for the insight which religion also promises: insight into the why and whither of our being here. Fiction is of the greatest significance in high culture, for the reason that fictional objects are creatures of the imagination. Hence, by pondering them, we free ourselves from our ordinary interests, and enter a realm where practical questions are not mine or yours or anyone's, but the imaginary questions of imaginary beings. Myth is the province of religion; but myth is not fiction, since it does not deal in imaginary worlds. It is received as a narrative of *this* world, but on a higher plane, in which individual characters are dissolved into archetypes, and accidents subsumed by fate. In the mythic narrative everything is typified, and both characters and actions lose their individuality. When the subject of the drama is individualised, myth becomes fiction – the presentation of *another* world, with all the specificity of this one.

Despite these differences, myth and high culture have much in common. Each is concerned to idealise the human condition,

---

3   I take the term 'imagined community' from Benedict Anderson, whose book is devoted to another but closely related question – the question of nationalism. (See Bibliography.)

to lift it free from contingencies, and to reveal the inner logic of our passions. Fictional characters are not archetypes but individuals: nevertheless, their characters are filtered through the screen of drama, and only what is typical stands out – typical of that individual, in that predicament. In fiction the dross of contingency is purged, and human life becomes a sign whose meaning is itself. In a high culture, fictional situations and characters are topics of meditation and instruction, as Odysseus was. They create a commentary on this world through thoughts of other worlds, where sympathy runs free. Yet the object of interest is always also here and now – the particular words, sounds, sights and gestures that are brought before us by the work of art. It is scarcely surprising, therefore, that there should attach to the products of a high culture the same sense of profound mystery and ineffable meaning that is the daily diet of religion. Our lives are transfigured in art, and redeemed of their arbitrariness, their contingency and littleness. This redemption occurs with no leap into the transcendental, no summoning of the god of the shrine, but simply in a purposeless encounter with a useless object. It therefore haunts us with its familiarity, its this-worldliness, its human pathos.

It seems to me that the art of our high culture – and not only of ours – has drawn upon and amplified the experiences which are given in less conscious form by religion: experiences of the sacred and the profane, of redemption from sin and the immersion in it, of guilt, sorrow and their overcoming through forgiveness and the one-ness of a community restored. Art has grown from the sacred view of life. And that is why art suddenly leapt into prominence at the Enlightenment, with the eclipse of sacred things. Thereafter art became a redeeming enterprise, and the artist stepped into the place vacated by the prophet and the priest. People began to dispute passionately over the difference between good art and bad, and to construct curricula whose sole contents were the masterpieces of a literary, musical or artistic tradition.

At this point you might object to the direction of my argument. Surely, you will say, to place art and religion in such proximity is to ignore their essential rivalry. Religion involves the expression and enforcement of a shared belief. It is a matter of faith and obedience. Art requires no common belief, but only an imaginative involvement with situations, characters, ideas and life-styles that may have no independent appeal. We can find beauty in works which grow from false religions, which express other cultures, and which reflect worldviews remote from ours. Indeed, on one plausible view, it is part of the value of art, that it causes us to widen our emotional horizons, by inducing imaginative sympathy with forms of life that run counter to our expectations. And you might go further, offering as one justification for Western civilisation that – thanks to the Enlightenment – it has emancipated art from religious usage, set it against the reign of prejudice, and created, by means of the imagination, a moral space – a place of freedom and experiment – that has never existed elsewhere.

You might also take exception to my argument from the religious perspective. To narrow the distance between art and religion, you might say, is to run the risk of aestheticising religion, so voiding it of faith and worship. It is to make an idol of art, and to demote the supremely important matter, which is faith and its moral sequel, to a subordinate position in the scheme of things. It is, to borrow Tom Paine's metaphor, to pity the plumage and forget the dying bird.

Two considerations might neutralise those objections. Faith and worship are the goals of religious practice, and for the believer they are ends in themselves. But to the anthropologist, looking on religion from a point of view outside it, faith and worship are means, not ends. Religion has a twofold social function: to establish the motives on which a community depends; and to teach the art of feeling. By sacralising the core experiences of society, religion eternalises our commitments, makes us admirable to one another, elevates the human person to the summit of creation, and gives sense and direction to our lives. It does this in a unique way, by offering to all-comers, whatever their education, the experience of sacred words and rituals. This experience transfigures human life, and imbues it with a long-term dutifulness. But it is available only through faith. It is outside the reach of the anthropologist, whose knowledge of the function of religion sets him at a distance from its doctrines. The function is fulfilled only by those who are ignorant of it, and who devote their attention to the gods.

Art too has a function – and it is closely related. Art ennobles the human spirit, and presents us with a justifying vision of ourselves, as something higher than nature and apart from it. It does this, not as religion does, by demanding belief and worship. For it engages our sympathies without compelling any doctrine. We are not *aware* of this function, unless subliminally. Nevertheless it informs our judgements, and causes us to evaluate works of art as more or less moving, more or less compelling, more or less serious. When a work of art conveys a view of things, our interest is not in the truth of that view, but in the extent to which it can be incorporated into a life of lasting commitment and serious feeling.

The point was made in other terms by T.S. Eliot, in an early essay on Shelley, and later, in *The Use of Poetry and the Use of Criticism,* where he tries to justify his low opinion of Shelley as a poet. Eliot criticises Shelley not for the atheistical views expressed in his poems – much as Eliot disapproved of them – but because these views are entertained in a puerile way. They are not put to the test, not given the kind of poetic examination which would show how a life of serious feeling could be built on them. They lack the seriousness and sincerity that would make them worthy of imaginative endorsement. Such, in a nutshell, is Eliot's answer to the problem of 'poetry and belief', and it seems to me to be the right one.

Furthermore, to say that the function of art lies close to that of religion is not to aestheticise religion. It is merely to notice – what is all-important to us, who live in a cynical age – that for those blessed by a high culture it is possible, though with ever-increasing difficulty, to retain the consoling vision which religion grants to all its supplicants. It is possible, through the complicitous web of feeling that a culture keeps in place, to look on the human spirit as a thing redeemed.

If those thoughts are true, then they help to explain the importance of tradition, and of its complement, originality. An artistic tradition is a constantly evolving system of conventions, allusions, cross-references and shared expectations. Themes, forms, ornaments and styles are things both inherited and invented, and the inheritance is part of what makes the invention possible. The successful work of art presents exemplary content in exemplary form; its character as an end implies that it is irreplaceable – there is no other work that will 'do just as well', since what it does is itself. Hence it is always there, never surpassed or replaced, always to be revisited. Inevitably, therefore, a high culture involves a repertoire, an accumulation of works of art and exemplary utterances, which create the common ground in which the new and the surprising are planted.

Words in a language owe their meaning to conventions, and we learn the language by internalising the rules. It is a convention of English that chickens are denoted by the word 'chicken', and not by 'poule' or 'dajajah'. Once in use, however, a word acquires meaning in another way, through the association of sound and sense, through colliding and consorting with other words in a language, through the literary works which exploit its expressive potential, and so on. Hence the English 'chicken' has an aura distinct from Arabic 'dajajah', and poems about chickens cannot be translated without loss of meaning from one language to the other.

Meaning in art does not arise from conventions or rules. On the contrary, conventions and rules arise from meaning. The meaning of a chord in music is not arbitrarily assigned like the meaning of a word, but attached by the magnetic force of context. Gradually, as chords are used and re-used, their musical potential becomes standardised; they become mossed over with allusions and reminiscences. It is only then that artistic conventions (like that of the twelve-bar blues) make sense: by exploiting and standardising a meaning that is achieved in another way. Moreover, art, unlike language, is intrinsically suspicious of this standardising process. Convention is tolerable only as a background to other and more individual meanings: if it becomes the foreground of the artistic enterprise, the result is cliché. The constant lapse into cliché, and the fastidious fear of it, are marks of a high culture in decline.

Allusion and elusiveness are as important in high culture as they are in the language and rites of a religion. To explain is to alienate: it is to show something as 'outside', observed but not internalised. It is to place conception above experience, as in science or historical research. Nothing is significant aesthetically, unless embodied in, and revealed through, experience. Hence the need for allusion, which imports a reference without describing it, so leaving the thread of pure experience unbroken. Moreover, allusions, unlike explanations, create a social context: common knowledge, common references, common symbols, embodied in an experience assumed also to be common. In grasping an allusion we enter a shared experience and an implied community.

An allusion is designed to be noticed: it expressly summons one work into the orbit of another. Allusions exploit familiarity and also create it, binding the high culture into a many-stranded web. Literary forms are themselves allusive: heroic couplets point the English reader to Pope and Dryden, as does the sonnet to Shakespeare, Donne and Wordsworth, while the unrhymed pentameters of Tennyson stand in the shadow of Wordsworth, looking constantly upwards to that source. The intentions of the author play with the expectations of the reader, and it is thus that a literary culture arises – a complex and communal game, but one of the highest seriousness, whose subject-matter is a shared experience of life.

This self-conscious act of sharing is essentially *critical* – it both idealises human emotion and also elicits sympathy; it therefore cannot escape judging and being judged. Is it right to sympathise, for example with Othello's final grief over the woman he has murdered (and in any case, is it really *grief* over *her*?)? An artistic tradition is an exercise of imagination; it is also an exercise of taste, which is in turn a meditation on human experience and an attempt to build a shared conception of what is worthy of our concern. The disgusting, the morbid, the banal and the sentimental are avoided, or not avoided only because unnoticed – which itself bespeaks a decline of taste. It is in epochs of cultural decline that criticism becomes important. Criticism is a last ditch attempt to be part of the artistic tradition, to retain the internal perspective on an inherited culture, and to fight off the corruption of sentiment that comes about, when cliché and sentimentality are mistaken for sincere expression. By eliciting sympathy towards empty forms, the cliché impoverishes the emotional life of those who are drawn to it. Hence the extreme vigilance with which modern critics try to draw the line between the genuine and the fake emotion. Whether they can succeed in this, is a question to which I return. Perhaps the distinction between the genuine and the fake is a fake.

Although artists borrow procedures, forms and repertoires, although they are contributing to a continuous and publicly validated enterprise, they can make no impact merely by copying what has already been done. The encounter with the individual is what makes art so supremely interesting: we, the audience, have set our interests aside, in order to open ourselves to what another person is, says and feels. It need not be new; but it must at least be *his*. A work is original to the extent that it *originates* in its creator. It shows us the world from his or her perspective, draws us into spheres which are not our own, and enables us to rehearse the possibilities of feeling on which an ideal community – a community of sympathy – is founded. Without originality the high culture will die, drooping into tired gestures and imitative rituals, like the worn-out ceremonies of a religion that is no longer believed.

Originality is not an attempt to capture attention come what may, or to shock or disturb in order to shut out competition from the world. The most original works of art may be genial applications of a well-known vocabulary, like the late quartets of Haydn, or whispered meditations like the Sonnets of Rilke. They may be all but unnoticeable amid the fanfares of contemporary self-advertisement, like the trapped interiors of Vuillard or the tucked-away churches of Borromini. What makes them original is not their defiance of the past or their rude assault on settled expectations, but the element of surprise with which they invest the forms and repertoire of a tradition. Without tradition, originality cannot exist: for it is only against a tradition that it becomes perceivable. Tradition and originality are two components of a single process, whereby the individual makes himself known through his membership of the historical group.

Although the aesthetic experience is central to high culture, it is not the only source upon which a culture draws. Any social in which we strive to give meaning to something as an end attracts to itself the community of sentiment for which we spontaneously hunger. Two significant instances of this are costumes and manners. In a flourishing high culture people dress not only for the utility of dressing, but also as a part of social display, signalling through their costumes their place in an idealised community, and representing their character and their social valency in the forms and colours of their clothes. Manners have a similar meaning: they too are part of representation, and although manners have a function, in binding communities together and smoothing the edges where friction occurs, the function is not the purpose. Only when manners are cultivated for their own sake, for the grace and good nature that are intrinsic to them, do they fulfil their function of oiling the social wheels. And when the function becomes the purpose, as in much modern business, manners become a thin pretence.

Still, it is the work of art which has, since the Enlightenment, provided our paradigm of high culture; and there is a reason for this. When a common culture declines, the ethical life can be sustained and renewed only by a work of the imagination. And that, in a nutshell, is why high culture matters.

5
Romanticism

The culture of Enlightenment, I argued, bears witness to a deep and recurring conflict. The free individual, motivated by reason, and guided by universal ideals, at the same time longs for community, for locality and for the warmth and protection of the tribe. Hence the era which saw the 'rational' reforms of the Emperor Joseph II in Austria, the Revolution in France, the birth of modern democracy in America, and the programmes for universal education, saw too the rise of the Masonic and Rosicrucian Orders, with their closed doors, their mysteries and their rites of passage. Study that sublime masterpiece of Masonic art – *The Magic Flute* of Mozart – and you will see that the two conflicting impulses of Enlightenment have a common emotional source.[1] The priest Sarastro, who offers freedom, truth, and the community of moral beings, is also an *excluder*, who offers these universal goods at the end of ordeals, and through mysteries which speak once again of the tribe, its comfort, and its all-enveloping darkness. The marriage of Pamino and Tamina is not a contract but a vow, the subject-matter of an elaborate rite which purges the individual of his wilfulness and subjects him to a moral order beyond the reach of reason. That which the Enlightenment drove from the public world – superstition, ceremony and the rites of the tribe – has been resurrected as a mystery, the exclusive property of the enlightened few. And, in a certain measure, this symbolises the role of high culture in the newly enlightened world.

At about the time of *The Magic Flute,* Goethe and Schiller were pondering the distinction between ancient and modern art. For Schiller the poetry of the Greeks was the voice of Nature.

---

1   Jacques Chailly, *The Magic Flute, Masonic Opera,* London 1972, and Nicholas Till, *Mozart and the Enlightenment,* London 1992, Chapter 18.

Through the verse of Homer the beauty and purity of man's childhood can be re-imagined. Such poetry – which Schiller called naïve – shows man at home in the natural world, whereas the 'sentimental' poetry of modern times is a poetry of *seeking,* in which Nature is invoked from afar.[2] Goethe likewise saw Greek art as imbued with a freedom, naturalness and order which have since gone from the world. In their place we have inwardness, sentiment and *Sehnsucht* – the longing that is never appeased.[3]

Already the terms 'classic' and 'romantic' were being used to contrast ancient and modern art, and by the time of Hegel's *Lectures on Aesthetics* (published posthumously between 1832 and 1840), the distinction was everywhere acknowledged as fundamental to the understanding of contemporary art and music. The Romantic movement defined itself in the terms made canonical by Hegel: as the exaltation of the subjective over the objective, and the inner yearning over the outward form. The lesser Romantics thought of themselves as reacting to the good taste and decorum of their predecessors; hence the term 'classical' soon came to denote both the art of the ancient Mediterranean, and also the poetry, painting and music of aristocratic Europe: specifically that of the late seventeenth and earlier eighteenth centuries. The greatest of the Romantics – Goethe, Schiller, Wordsworth, Beethoven, Schubert and Keats – were, in this sense, also classical. They were masters of the Enlightenment styles, expressing the haunted longings of the artist with the clarity and melodiousness which they admired in ancient poetry and sculpture.

Romanticism was less a reaction to the Enlightenment than an attitude concealed within it. Only against the background of emancipation does the poetic *Weltschmerz* make sense. In the

---

2   *Über naïve und sentimentalische Dichtung:* see bibliography.

3   The *locus classicus* here is Goethe's *Italienische Reise,* and the character of Mignon in *Wilhelm Meister.* It is interesting to note that Goethe projected, but never finished, a drama on the theme of Elpenor (the unwitting hero of my Chapter 2, where I give a modern anthropological version of what Schiller and Goethe were getting at).

lasting monuments of Romantic art we encounter the art-ist-hero, for whom freedom is both an absolute value and an intolerable burden. In plumbing the depths of his soul he is also, like Beethoven in his late quartets and the Choral Symphony, like Wordsworth in the *Prelude,* like Hölderlin in his poems of travel, invoking the community which he offends through his transgression, and to which he will somehow mysteriously come home. The course of Romantic art is one of ever deeper mourning for the life of 'natural piety' which Enlightenment destroyed. And from this mourning springs the Romantic hope – the hope of recreating in imagination the community that will never again exist in fact. Hence the importance of folk poetry, folk traditions, and 'ancestral voices'. Beneath the rational culture of Enlightenment, the Romantics searched for another and deeper culture – the culture of the people, rooted in mystery, and surviving in the inner sanctuary of the poet's self.

It is appropriate that the first attempt to give form to this 'folk' culture was a fabrication, recognised as such by that great champion of the classical spirit, Dr Johnson. Macpherson's *Poems of Ossian* purported to be translated from a Gaelic original; in fact it invented a lost community of heroes, in which nature and man were in harmony, in which human life was idealised and sanctified, and in which the burden of freedom was happily put down. The Scottish Border ballads, Herder's anthology of folk poetry, von Arnim and Brentano's *Das Knaben Wunderhorn* – all such collections were put together as much from bourgeois dreams and parlour games as from real folk traditions. But that only testifies to the power of the longing which inspired them – the longing inimitably captured by Mozart in his last operatic masterpiece, for the rites of passage that would rescue us from freedom, by making freedom into a new form of membership.

In the last chapter I pointed to the ascendancy of the aesthetic in Enlightenment thinking. It is precisely this which made the Romantic movement possible. For the aesthetic attitude is already a kind of mourning. It places a frame around its object and looks upon it as something spiritual, transfigured – and therefore dead. The primary object of aesthetic experience, for Kant, was nature, and in the aestheticising of nature we glimpse the Romantic movement in its deepest impulse. Nature had ceased to be the unnoticed background to life, and become instead an object of concern. The eighteenth century identified nature through the picturesque – in other words, through its image in art. The woods and vales celebrated in Augustan poetry were self-evidently the work of man, and bore the imprint of a way of life. The aesthetic gaze which freezes these things intends thereby to immortalise the life which produced them. The search for natural beauty is at the same time an attempt to preserve the old way of life – the rooted, pious, unquestioning and obedient life – which Enlightenment inevitably destroys.

This complex attitude to the natural world has survived into our time, and lies at the heart of our culture. The natural beauty of the English countryside, invoked and lamented by the poets, painters and composers of our century, resides precisely in those features that memorialise a vanished industry: the hedgerows, copses, bridleways, green lanes, stone walls, barns and cottages tell of small-scale farming, mixed crops and the warm proximity of dependent animals. We cannot, it seems, protect that way of life from modern agribusiness; but we strive nevertheless to conserve its visible record. The aesthetic gaze immortalises, and sees in every change the threat of desecration.

In Romantic art, therefore, nature gains a new importance. It is the supremely threatened thing, the long-lost home from which we have been sundered, the symbol of an Edenic innocence that manufacture, materialism and Enlightenment have jointly destroyed. From Wordsworth to Hopkins, from Beethoven to Vaughan Williams, from Constable to Cézanne, the image of nature returns with its promise of a more than worldly consolation. And invariably it is associated with membership in its vanished or vanishing forms: the pious routines and rites of passage of a folk culture at peace with itself.

From the very beginning of the Romantic movement, however, consciousness stands *apart* from the natural world. The Romantic artist is a wanderer. The old moral order that lies enfolded in nature has withdrawn from his grasp. Goethe's Faust typifies this stance, and nothing is more prophetic of the course of modern culture than Faust's relation to Gretchen, the innocent girl whom he casts from the orbit of her natural piety. Mephistopheles transports Faust, who has encountered Gretchen only in the street, into the girl's virginal room. As he rhapsodises over the innocent life that surrounds him, Faust throws himself into an old leather armchair, a *Väterthron* (throne of fathers), as he describes it, and imagines the generations of children who had played around it, the grandfather's hand kissed in gratitude by Gretchen, the motherly routines of the young maid, as she busies herself in furnishing her home. The passage (lines 2687–2728) is saturated with the thought of reproduction: father, grandfather, mother, children – all pass in delirium through the rapturous verses, as Faust contemplates the life that he is about to destroy.

Goethe accurately identifies in this passage the source of the Romantic *Weltschmerz*. Fulfilment for Gretchen lies in marriage, which will confer full membership in her closed community. All the sublime artifice which shows itself as artless simplicity and tender concern, has been but a preparation for the rite of passage, the vow that will bind her to the father of her children. But Faust's love removes her from the sphere of natural piety, and makes of her an aesthetic ideal. Precisely because she belongs to that old world, the world before Enlightenment, she is unobtainable, a creature of the imagination, who is etherealised and placed out of reach. What is obtained is not Gretchen, for whom faithful marriage is the only goal, but the debauched remnant of Gretchen, the body in which the soul is no more than an anxious memory, and which is cast loose from the moral order.

The theme is a *Leitmotif* of Romantic literature. Consciousness lies outside the moral order, observing, regretting, tragically sundered from the thing that it would possess. But possession, when it comes, is both supremely erotic and also a desecration, a removal of the object from its domestic shrine. The tragedy of Enlightenment is enacted in every erotic adventure, as love runs free from marriage to become a personal acquisition, a mark of distinction, with no rite of passage into the moral community. From object to object the observing consciousness wanders, never satisfied, never at home, animated by an incurable nostalgia which feeds on beauty wherever it is found. This is the experience humorously recorded by Byron in *Don Juan,* and warned against in the sagacious novels of Jane Austen.

Three themes therefore dominate Romantic art: nature, erotic love, and the world before Enlightenment. And the three belong together. Each presents a haven for the pilgrim soul, a place of refuge and homecoming. But it is an unreal refuge: aestheticised, removed from the material world, and frequented by ghosts. The landscape is not a means of production, but an elaborate tomb, a monument to the vanished world of piety. Erotic love offers a vista into that world, but it is no more than a vista: the passage back to the moral order has been closed and the rites discarded. The world before Enlightenment is also etherealised; it is a 'dream of fair women', a gothic shrine where pre-Raphaelite females bless the visitor with wan insipid smiles. By the time of Tennyson the romantic dream is supremely conscious of its emptiness. In *Morte d'Arthur* the dying king is all of us, and the hand which rises from the lake – 'clothed in white samite, mystic, wonderful' – waves farewell from the tribe. Once or twice thereafter we hear 'the horns of elfland faintly blowing' – in Mahler, in Vaughan Williams, in Walter de la Mare, even in Stefan George. But the Romantic movement is over.

The Romantic period was artistically the richest that our civilisation has known. To summarise its achievement is a task far beyond my present purpose or ability. Nevertheless, we should try to understand the ambivalence that modern people feel towards the Romantic impulse, since it has helped to shape both modernism in the arts and modern culture generally. The high culture of the Enlightenment, as I described it, involved a noble and energetic attempt to rescue the ethical view of human life – the view of life which flourished spontaneously in the old religious culture, but which demanded to be snatched from the ruins, when that culture collapsed. The rescue was a work of the imagination, in which the aesthetic attitude took over from religious worship as the source of intrinsic values. And the greatest artistic achievements of the Enlightenment fulfil the promise that inspired them. In Mozart, Goethe, Schiller, Blake and Rousseau the ethical vision of our nature outlasts the closed community. Thereafter art becomes a continuous meditation on our loss

– a melancholy acknowledgement that the primary source of moral feeling has dried up, and that *only* the aesthetic remains. Subjected to the extreme pressures of a secular and materialistic way of life, art begins to compromise, to lose itself in wishful thinking and in dreams. Ready-made fantasies replace the work of imagination, and firm moral sentiment gives way to vapid sentimentality. The romantic hero begins to lose confidence in the ethical vision which created him. Like Byron's Don Juan he begins to glory in his isolation, and to use his outsider status in order to disrupt the membership enjoyed by other and more innocent people.[4] Erotic love becomes a destructive force, precisely because its true object is imagined, etherealised, and rendered unobtainable. Thereafter marriage is seen more as a bourgeois weakness than as the sacred rite of passage upon which the ethical life depends. The ethical vision, entrusted to the aesthetic gaze, is bit by bit betrayed by it.

In a remarkable and prescient work the Danish philosopher Søren Kierkegaard foretold this process, invoking marriage as the core of ethical life, and the foundation of enduring communities. *Either/Or* (published in 1843) presents the Romantic yearning in the form of a dilemma. In the first part is invoked the aesthetic way of life, in which the moment is elevated above all long-term commitments, and duty surrendered to delight. Mozart's Don Juan is the acknowledged hero, and the centre piece is the celebrated 'Diary of a Seducer', in which an innocent girl falls under the aesthetic gaze of a writer for whom her innocence is both a promise of redemption and a challenge to destroy. In the second part a mild mannered judge moralises over the ethical life, and spells out the dull routines of marriage as the true redemption: the passage to community upon which life depends.

There is no doubt where Kierkegaard's sympathies lay. The unutterable tediousness of the 'Or' contrasts with the intellectual, poetic and – yes – *ethical* exhilaration of the 'Either'; and the reader is not surprised to learn that Kierkegaard himself, pressed to marry the girl whose life he had ruined by his promises, would never give 'yes' for an answer.

---

4   I am here trying to summarize a phenomenon described in another but related way by Mario Praz, in *The Romantic Agony*.

Kierkegaard was nevertheless a deeply religious man, and his exploration of the aesthetic way of life should be seen against the background of his faith in the Christian God. His attitude to faith was itself a distillation of the Romantic yearning. For Kierkegaard faith is profoundly irrational, a leap into the unknown, a gesture of complete 'subjectivity' in which the norms of Enlightenment are cast peremptorily aside. Indeed, if a word could summarise the peculiar character of Kierkegaard's Christian commitment, it would be 'aesthetic'. The plea for the ethical way of life is an elaborate sham. Like his contemporaries, the philosopher saw the aesthetic as the one true path to man's redemption, the posture towards the world which preserved, as best it could, the ethical vision which makes sense of our time on earth. In dressing up the aesthetic gaze in the attributes of holiness, Kierkegaard showed us the meaning of high culture.

While the high culture of our civilisation meditated on its spiritual legacy it became, as in Tennyson, more and more remote from the real world, more and more Arcadian and dreamlike. The real world was the world of commerce and manufacture. It had its own culture, in which advertising and salesmanship were more important than art or meditation. If we are to understand the modern movement – the originating impulse of modern culture – we should not see it as a reaction to Romanticism, but as the final shocked awakening of high culture to the truth of the modern world – the world in which everything, the sacred included, is for sale.

6
Fantasy, Imagination and the Salesman

The commercialisation of modern life has been the subject of lamentation ever since it was first remarked upon, and ambitious theories – commodity fetishism, conspicuous consumption, the affluent society, and countless lesser attempts[1] – have arisen from the natural revulsion that intellectuals feel towards the 'getting and spending' of others. But something new seems to be at work in the contemporary world – a process that is eating away the very heart of social life, not merely by putting salesmanship in place of moral virtue, but by putting everything – virtue included – on sale. The cynic, said Oscar Wilde, is the one who knows the price of everything and the value of nothing. And in a letter to Lord Alfred Douglas he described sentimentality as 'the bank holiday of cynicism'.[2] Wilde's quips tend to be more exciting than truthful. These, however, are exact. Cynicism and sentimentality are two ways in which things of value are demoted to things with a price.

To understand this we need to make a distinction that was first hinted at by Coleridge: the distinction between fantasy and imagination.[3] Both fantasy and imagination concern unrealities; but while the unrealities of fantasy penetrate and pollute the world, those of the imagination exist in a world of their own, in which we wander freely and in full knowledge of the really real.

---

1   Commodity fetishism: see Marx, *Capital,* vol. 1; conspicuous consumption: see Thorstein Veblen, *Theory of the Leisure Class,* Chicago 1899; affluent society: see J.K. Galbraith, *The Affluent Society,* New York 1958.

2   Oscar Wilde, ed. Rupert Hart-Davis, *The Letters of Oscar Wilde,* London 1967, p. 501.

3   Coleridge's distinction is between 'fancy' and imagination, and is delivered here and there in *Biographia Literaria.*

An example will establish what I mean. A morbid person may reflect endlessly on death and suffering. The image of agony is often before his mind. There is born in him the desire to witness what he so vividly imagines. At the same time fear, sympathy and the respect for human life make his desire abhorrent to him. He is not a torturer or a murderer, nor would he frequent the dark places where torture and murder occur. He looks instead for surrogates: the lifelike waxworks of the 'chamber of horrors', the realistic deaths and dismemberments in the films of Quentin Tarantino, and then – at the limit – the 'snuff' movie in which actual death is delivered but from another sphere, removed from all prevention. This process shows fantasy at work. The fantasy object intrudes into the real world: it is an unreal object of an actual desire, condemned to unreality by the mental prohibition that also summons it. The fantasy object must be as realistic as possible, in order to provide the surrogate for which the subject craves. Fantasy covets the gross, the explicit, the no-holds-barred display of the unobtainable; and in the crisis of display the unobtainable is vicariously obtained.

Hard-core pornography provides another instance. Indeed, modern society abounds in fantasy objects, since the realistic image, in photograph, cinema and TV screen, offers surrogate fulfilment to all our forbidden desires, thereby permitting them. A fantasy desire seeks neither a literary description, nor a delicate painting of its object, but a simulacrum – the nearest alternative to the thing itself. It eschews style and convention, since these impede the building of the surrogate, and veil it in thought. The ideal fantasy is perfectly realised, and perfectly unreal – an imaginary object which leaves nothing to the imagination. Advertisements trade in such objects, and they float in the background of modern life, a chorus of disconsolate ghosts. Observe the eager queue at Madame Tussaud's, the waxwork museum in London, and you will understood how ubiquitous is the force of fantasy, and how easily satisfied. No effort of the imagination is required to understand a wax-work. It stands amid the wash of easy sentiment, and is never corroded. It is the paradigm fantasy object: absolutely lifelike, and absolutely dead. Through the work of art, by contrast, we encounter a world of real, vulnerable and living people, which we can enter only by an effort of the imagination, and where we, like they, are on trial. (Hence there are no comparable queues outside the National Gallery.)

The matter of imagination is not realised but *represented*; it comes to us, as a rule, heavily masked by thought, and in no sense is it a surrogate, standing in place of the unobtainable. On the contrary, it is deliberately placed at a distance, in a world of its own. The obvious examples of this – theatre and painting – tell us also that convention, framing and restraint are integral to the imaginative process. We enter the painting only by recognising that the frame shuts out the world in which we stand. Convention and style are more important than realisation; and when a painter endows his image with a *trompe-l'oeil* reality, we question the result as tasteless or despise it as kitsch. In the theatre too, the action is not real but represented, and however realistic, stops short of realising those scenes which are the food of fantasy.

Hence in Greek tragedy the murders took place off stage, not in order to deny their emotional power, but in order to contain it within the domain of imagination – the domain where we wander freely, with our own interests and desires in abeyance. The Greeks well knew what our *cinéastes* have since discovered – that the portrayal of sex and violence is the natural object of fantasy, and slides of its own accord from realism to realisation. Hence it disrupts the work of the imagination, which engages our sympathies, but not our real desires.

What is represented in the theatre does not happen on the stage, nor anywhere else in the world that we inhabit. Nor do educated observers think otherwise. They perceive what is going on, and perceive it as imaginary. Coleridge described the posture of the reader (and therefore of the spectator in the theatre) as a 'willing suspension of disbelief'.[4] He should have written a 'willing suspension of belief': all pleasure and emotion depend on knowing that the action on stage is unreal. And the spectators enter this unreality by an act of will, not in search of surrogates for their own desires, but in order to explore a world that is not their own.

Hence, although fantasy constantly intrudes on the real

---

4   *Ibid.*, Ch. 14.

world, and gains its credentials from desire, it also *undermines* reality. The fantasy-ridden person has a diminished sense of the objectivity of his world, and of his own agency within it. The habit of pursuing the 'realised unreal' veils the really real, blocking out demands and difficulties. In fantasy the object of desire loses the ability to withhold itself. And since gratification through fantasy is without apparent cost, it is endlessly repeated; desire invades the world and cancels the world's demands. The character of the fantasy object, moreover, is entirely dictated by the desire which seeks for it – the object is tailor-made, the perfect dummy, the walking talking Barbie-doll who does what I want since my wanting and her doing are one and the same.

Although the passions suffered in the theatre are imaginary, they are guided by a sense of reality. The passions of the imagination do not precede their object; they are responses to imagined situations, and evolve and develop as our understanding grows. They derive from the sympathy that we feel for our kind, and sympathy is critical – it wishes to know its object, to assess its worth, and not to waste its heart-beats undeservedly.

The contrast here can be easily seen in the distinction between pornography and erotic art. The pornographic image is designed both to arouse sexual appetite, and to provide it with a surrogate object. The girl encountered in the image is the object of *my* desire, miraculously offered on a plate, without the impediment of real existence, and slavishly obedient to the lust that she arouses. The girl in the erotic painting is not the object of my desire, but only of imaginary desires in an imaginary world. And in that world she is real and resistant, as much a person as any other, whose sexual favours must be purchased by risk, adventure and respect. Erotic art aims to prompt not real desire but a meditative sympathy with the desires of imagined beings. Hence erotic art, unlike pornography, may be nuptial, dignified and chaste, in the manner of a Titian Venus.

The emotions inspired by serious art belong to imagination, not to fantasy. And that is why it is often so difficult to describe them. In the normal case emotion depends upon belief – as fear depends upon the belief that I am in danger, and anger on the belief that I have been wronged. When belief is suspended, ordinary emotions lose their foundation. A desire that arises from an imaginative thought is not a real desire: and without real desire, there is no real emotion. I no more desire Othello not to murder Desdemona than I desire to leave the theatre, even though murder is, in this imaginary world, as terrible as murders really are. In such a case desire is not felt, but 'entertained', just as the thought of what is happening is not believed but held in suspension.

In a sense it is even wrong to say that it is *I* who feel grief over Desdemona's fate. I imagine such a grief, and am drawn into sympathy with the thing that I imagine. We might say that here there is neither real object nor real feeling, but a response in imagination to an imagined scene. In fantasy, by contrast, there is a real feeling which fixes upon an unreal object, in order to gratify vicariously what cannot be gratified in fact.

Since imaginative emotions are responses, they are determined by their imaginary objects. They arise out of, and are controlled by, an understanding of the world. And to exercise this understanding is to take an interest in truth. The questions arise: are things really like that? Is it plausible? Is my response exaggerated? Am I being invited to feel what I should not feel? Such questions are the life of imagination, and also the death of fantasy, which withers as soon as its object is granted independent life or subjected to interrogation.

For similar reasons, we can say that 'realisation', the creation of a surrogate or simulacrum, is not the main aim of imaginative thought, and may even impede it. The imagination, governed as it is by a sense of reality, seeks condensation, suggestion, dramatic completeness. The absolute realisation of specific scenes is no part of the imaginative purpose, which is better served by convention than explicit imagery.

But although imagination is, in this way, informed by a sense of reality, it need not represent the world as it is. On the contrary – the imagination idealises, ennobles, embellishes and re-presents the world. And it does so in a believable way, since (paradoxically) we can suspend belief only in the presence of the believable. Aristotle made the point in the *Poetics*. Poetry, he argued, does not tolerate the improbable, but it can tolerate the impossible, provided the impossible is also believable (as Ovid's impossible metamorphoses are believable).

The ennobling power of the imagination lies in this: that it re-orders the world, and re-orders our feelings in response to it. Fantasy, by contrast, is frequently degrading. For it begins from the premise of a given emotion, which it can neither improve nor criticise but only feed. It is a slave of the actual, and deals in forbidden goods. Where imagination offers glimpses of the sacred, fantasy offers sacrilege and profanation.

It is helpful here to revisit the oldest of religious controversies: that concerning idolatry. The idol is a mundane object mistaken for a god: in focusing our religious feelings on an idol we profane what is most sacred, namely the act of worship, which is our only reliable link with the transcendental. The emotional disorder involved in this has been beautifully conveyed by Poussin, in his painting of the *Golden Calf* (National Gallery, London). The foreground is dominated by the calf, raised on its pedestal. The idol is a glowing surrogate, life-like but dead, with the emphatic deadness of metal. Aaron gestures with priestly pride to his creation, while the people, drunk, helpless and in the grip of collective delusion, dance like brainless animals around this thing less sacred than themselves. In focusing on the calf their emotions are also out of focus – bewildered, diseased, gyrating in a void. In the distance, barely visible, is the figure of Moses, descending from Mount Sinai with the tables of the law: the abstract decrees of an abstract God, who can be understood through no earthly image but only through law. Moses casts the stone tablets to the ground, destroying thereby not the law but its earthly record. The contrast here is between the active work of imagination, which points to a God beyond the sensory world, and the passive force of fantasy, which creates its own god out of sensory desires. Every idol is also a sacrilege, since it causes us to focus the worship that is due to higher things on something lower than ourselves. Only by responding to what is higher than the human, do we become truly human.

The fear of sacrilege is an essential part of religion. And the reason for this should be apparent from what was said in Chapter 2. The central concern of every religion is the *focus* of human emotion – and especially of those emotions which sustain the community. There are certain things which can be properly confronted only through solemn rituals, whereby absent generations shore up our human frailty. One such thing is death. Our feelings veer away from death, since it seems to deny all that we are. But by focusing beyond the sensory world – the world in which death occurs – we deprive death of its sting. The threat of nothingness is averted, and the community re-forms itself, as the dead person, by means of the ritual, passes to a higher place among his kind. The idea of the sacred performs a vital role in this transition: it focuses emotion beyond the immediate fact, and so enables us both to overcome our fears and at the same time to confront what has happened. By focusing on sacred things, we give the human world its proper weight, and experience it completely. By focusing on profane things, we ruin what is sacred. We subject the world to our fears and foibles, and take a step back from the true community towards self-isolation.

A telling illustration of this is the ceremony of marriage. In the Christian religion marriage is a sacrament – in other words, a relation that can be completed only by God.[5] Marriage is not a contract, but a vow before God, undertaken in the sacred presence. Bride and bridegroom consecrate their lives, and this consecration is a sacrifice: their lives are henceforth given to something higher than themselves, and the privations of fidelity, mutual aid and childbearing are undertaken for eternity.

The shift in perspective from the sacred to the secular view of human institutions naturally changed all that. The Enlightenment brought with it an attempt to remake the marriage bond as a contract for mutual benefit – if not quite 'a contract for the mutual use of the sexual organs', as Kant described it in the *Lectures on Ethics*. There followed a brave but brief attempt to rescue marriage from the market, through the propagation of

---

5   Whether this was always so may be doubted. The Church did not describe marriage as a sacrament until the Renaissance, when the other forms of sacramental life – the monastic and the priestly – were on the wane: see Lawrence Stone, *The Family, Sex and Marriage in England, 1500–1800,* London 1977, p.31. However, the idea of marriage as a 'vow before God' precedes the ceremonial recognition of this status.

heroic ideals of mutual support and sacrifice.[6] But we now know that the long-term effect of secularisation has been the gradual erosion of marriage, as a distinct form of human commitment: in place of it has come the defeasible contract for mutual profit. God has no part in the arrangement, and solemnity is a state-sponsored sham. As a result the sacrificial aspect of marriage has disappeared: people no longer consecrate their lives through marriage, and discard their obligations just as soon as a better deal appears. Reflect on this, and what it means for the reproduction of the community, and you will see how valuable the idea of the sacred was, and how intimate is the connection, not only in etymology, but also in fact, between the sacred, the sacrificial and the consecrated.

In the religious ceremony of marriage, the words uttered by bride and groom have a supernatural power. Although they have been spoken by every couple who were ever joined by them, it is as though they are being spoken here and now for the first time. Like spells, they create what they describe, and the vow becomes an eternal echo of the frail and mortal voice that utters it. Deny the sacred presence and the focus shifts to a man and a woman, and the words between them are no longer vows but defeasible promises, which can be cancelled when the parties choose. The words then lose their solemnity, become commonplace, trite and stilted, like the pseudo-antique jargon in a legal document.

Max Weber wrote in this connection of the progressive 'disenchantment' – *Entzauberung* – of social life. Places, times and actions lose their holiness, the gods retreat from us, and our bonds are sealed by no higher force than law. And this is what we must expect when religion dies, and the common culture evaporates like a mist beneath the sun of reason. It is in just these circumstances, I have argued, that imagination acquires its modern role – the role of ennobling, spiritualising, re-presenting humanity as something higher than itself.

But the shift in focus which threatens religion can occur also in a disenchanted world. Humanity itself may be profaned, and will be profaned when fantasy takes charge of human dealings.

---

6   See the illuminating discussion of *Le nozze di Figaro,* in Nicholas Till, *Mozart and the Enlightenment,* London 1992, pp 140–171.

The second commandment makes idolatry a sin; but it also warns us against more modern vices. For the surrogate human is as dangerous as the surrogate god, and the demeaning habit of fantasy erodes all higher feelings.

Pornography again illustrates what is at stake. The pornographic image is essentially de-personalising; its function is to 'market' sexual gratification, by attaching it to an impersonal surrogate. The focus is on the sexual act and the sexual organs, detached from any personal relationship. In other words, pornography effects a shift in focus – a shift downwards from the human person, the object of love and desire, to the human animal, the object of lustful fantasies – from the face which is you to the sex which is everyone. As in the case of idolatry, the shift in focus is also a profanation. By focusing on the wrong things we pollute and diminish the right things. In pornography, desire is detached from love, and attached to the mute machinery of sex. This is as much a profanation of erotic love as dancing around a golden calf is a profanation of divine worship.

As I have argued, fantasy replaces the real, resistant, objective world with a pliant surrogate. And it is important to see why this matters. Life in the actual world is difficult and embarrassing. Most of all is it difficult and embarrassing in our confrontation with other people who, by their very existence, make demands that we may be unwilling to meet. It requires a great force, a desire that fixes upon an individual, and sees that individual as unique and irreplaceable, if people are to make the sacrifices upon which the community depends for its longevity. It is far easier to take refuge in surrogates, which neither embarrass us nor resist our cravings. The habit grows of creating a compliant world of desire, in which the erotic force is dissipated and the needs of love denied.

Fantasies are private property, which I can dispose according to my will, with no answerability to the other. If they fill my mind in the act of love, then they constitute an abuse of the other, who has become the replaceable means to a self-regarding pleasure, rather than the object of an individualising desire. For the fantasist, therefore, the ideal partner is the rent-boy or the prostitute, whose purchasability solves at once the moral problem presented by the existence of another person at the scene of sexual release. Being purchasable, the prostitute is exchangeable, and therefore not truly *present* in the moment of desire. She is the universal absence which fantasy fills with substitute goods.

The connection between pornography and prostitution is witnessed by etymology. The effect of pornographic fantasy is to 'commodify' the object of desire, and to replace love and its vestigial sacraments with the law of the market. This is the final disenchantment of the human world. When sex becomes a commodity, the most important sanctuary of human ideals becomes a market, and value is reduced to price.

Fantasies of violence have a similar function: they obliterate the human person, by enlarging the human body, until it fills the foreground of our thoughts. This too involves a malignant shift of focus, and this too is a profanation. By focusing on the tortured body, we degrade the embodied person. In both sex and death we confront the mystery of our incarnation; and the temptation is to shift our focus from the embodied soul to the disanimated body, from the irreplaceable source of value, to the repeatable and transferable routine.

A comparable shift of focus occurs in sentimentality. And sentimentality plays a central role in modern culture – it is the mask with which fantasy conceals its cynical self-regard.

Sentimental feeling is easy to confuse with the real thing, for, on the surface at least, they have the same object. The sentimental love of Judy and the real love of Judy are both directed towards Judy, and involve tender thoughts of which she is the subject. But this superficial similarity marks a deep difference. The real *focus* of my sentimental love is not Judy but *me*. For the sentimentalist it is not the object but the subject of emotion that is important. Real love focuses on the other: it is gladdened by his pleasure and grieved by his pain. The unreal love of the sentimentalist focuses on the self, and treats the pleasures and pains of its object only as an excuse for playing the role that most appeals to it. It may seem to grieve at the other's sorrow, but it does not really grieve. For secretly sentimentalists welcome the sorrow that prompts their tears. It is another excuse for the noble gesture, another occasion to contemplate the image of a great-hearted self.

Hence the mark of sentimentality in art is a singular failure to *observe*. The critic F.R. Leavis has argued the point in a striking series of essays, taking apart the vast human pretence that lies at the heart of so much Victorian poetry – and of the lyrics of Tennyson in particular.[7] The object of grief in Tennyson's *In Memoriam*, for example, is only schematically identified: he is given no reality, no concretion, is quickly drowned by the flood of sentiment. Indeed, he hardly appears in the poem – for stanza upon stanza he has no definition, since the grieving poet stands too hugely between him and the light. The dead man has been shorn of all human reality, all rough contingency and imperfection; he flits in the shadow of the poet's great emotion, a thing unobserved. A favourite dog might have done just as well: as in pornography, the object of sentimental feeling is substitutable, is indeed a substitute for himself, a reconstruction in fantasy from which the embarrassing individuality has been deleted. When Hallam finally enters, it is as a holiday companion, reclining in the grass with a flask of wine beside him, a figure of Arcadian dreams. All of which, of course, is another way of saying that the source of the emotion is *not* Hallam at all, but Tennyson. This is not to disparage the beautiful descriptions with which this poem abounds or to deny its technical mastery. But it is to imply that Tennyson's evocations hide an emptiness of feeling – an emptiness revealed in language which protests too much that it feels.

Sentimentality and fantasy go hand in hand. For the object of sentimental emotion is, like a fantasy object, deprived of objective reality, made pliant to a subjective need, and roughly discarded when the going gets tough. He is, from the beginning, only an excuse for an emotion whose focus lies elsewhere, in the great drama of which the sentimentalist is the sole enduring hero. Hence the object of sentimental love is given no security, and will find himself quickly replaced in his lover's affections when the script requires it. The sentimental lover of Judy pretends to acknowledge her value; but in fact he has assigned her a price.

Sentimentality, like fantasy, is at war with reality. It

---

7   See especially 'Reality and Sincerity' and 'Thought and Emotional Quality', reprinted from *Scrutiny*, in F.R. Leavis, ed., *Selections from Scrutiny*, vol. 2, Cambridge 1966.

consumes our finite emotional energies in self-regarding ways and numbs us to the world of other people. It atrophies our sympathies, by guiding them into worn and easy channels, and so destroys not only our ability to feel, but also our ability to bring help where help is needed and to take risks on behalf of higher things. It may seem to project and endorse a vision of those higher things, to take on itself some of the ennobling function which is the imagination's proper task. But the appearance is an illusion. The object of sentimental emotion is in fact dragged down by the feeling which makes use of it, made grubby and tawdry in the game of emotional exchange. Sentimentality is another form of profanation. While pornography puts our sexual appetites on sale, sentimentality trades in love and virtue. But the effect is the same – to deprive these higher things of all reality, either by cynically denying them, or by making them insubstantial, dream-like and schematic.

This returns us to the question of 'poetry and belief'. When religion dies, I argued, the vision of man's higher nature is conserved by art. But art cannot be a substitute for religion, nor does it fill the void that is left by faith. Works of the imagination do not provide us with doctrines, or recruit us to the religious life, and if they try to do these things we stand back from them in rightful suspicion. The imagination can show us *what it is like* to believe some doctrine, and *what it is like* to follow customs and rituals that may be strange to us and alien; and in doing so it can awaken sympathy for emotions, beliefs and ways of life that are not and could not be ours. But it does not impart these things or impose them as a moral norm. The aesthetic understanding is tolerant, expansive, open to all that awakens sympathy. It interrogates the world, not as religion interrogates, in order to sniff out heresy and error, but in order to spread itself in sympathy. True religious poetry, like that of George Herbert, can be appreciated by the unbeliever. For it conveys an emotion which the reader can imaginatively share. Indeed, the greatness of Herbert lies in the innocent sincerity with which he expresses his doubts, his waywardness, and his joyful reunion with his Saviour. We can all enter into these feelings: the poems make them real to us, objects of a human concern, and petitioners for sympathy. If we speak of the truthfulness of Herbert's poems, we do not mean the truth of the religious doctrine that gave rise to them, but the sincerity with which they convey the religious drama. 'Truth' here means 'truth to life' – or rather, truth to the higher form of life which human beings manifest, when they live from sincere conviction.

A high culture may survive the religion that gave rise to it. But it cannot survive the triumph of fantasy, cynicism and sentimentality. For these re-focus our emotions. They cheapen our endeavours, by directing them away from what is serious, long-term and committed, towards what is immediate, effortless and for sale. A common culture dignifies people, by setting their desires and projects within an enduring context. It makes the spirit believable and commitment sincere, by providing the words, gestures, rituals and beliefs which moralise our actions. A high culture attempts to keep these things alive, by giving imaginative reality to the long-term view of things, and by setting us in the context of an imagined redemption.

But in the absence of a common culture the pursuit of meaning begins to appear strenuous, fruitless and absurd. From within the high culture there arises a spirit of repudiation, a desire, in D.H. Lawrence's words, 'to do dirt on life'. Every avenue to the spirit is sentimentalised, lest it should appear to make demands on us. And a cold-hearted cynicism begins to take hold of human speech. Art itself turns against the vestiges of culture, and morbid fantasies occupy the foreground of thought. Such is our situation. But it is a new situation, and one that our high culture has until now vigorously resisted. Indeed, the attempt to guard the sanctuary of sentiment against the salesman, and to shut the door in his face, is the true explanation of the most distinctive feature of modern culture – the movement in art, music and literature that we know as 'modernism'.

7
Modernism

In a world where everything is for sale, where value is price and price is value, where feelings are bartered, and the sentimental fake no longer distinguished from the genuine article, the artist becomes a modernist, and culture escapes to a garrett, high above the market place. For a century or more modern culture has been a modernist culture, and even if we are now entering a 'post-modern', or 'post-modernist', or maybe 'post-post-modernist' phase, there is no chance of understanding where we are without considering the modernist enterprise.

Three great artists prepared the way for modernism – Baudelaire, Manet and Wagner. And all three haunt the work of T.S. Eliot, the greatest modernist writer in English, and the one who has inspired the thoughts contained in this book. To begin with Wagner is not to begin the story of modernism at the beginning. But it is to gain insight into the mission bequeathed by the Enlightenment to art. The operas of Wagner attempt to dignify the human being in something like the way that he might be dignified by an uncorrupted common culture. Acutely conscious of the death of God, Wagner proposed man as his own redeemer and art as the transfiguring rite of passage to a higher world. The suggestion was visionary, and its impact on modern culture so great that the shock waves are still overtaking us. Modern high culture is as much a set of footnotes to Wagner as Western philosophy is, in Whitehead's judgement, footnotes to Plato.

In the mature operas of Wagner our civilisation gave voice for the last time to its idea of the heroic, through music which strives to endorse that idea to the full extent of its power. And because Wagner was a composer of supreme genius, perhaps the only one to have taken forward the intense inner language forged by Beethoven and to have used it to conquer the psychic spaces that Beethoven shunned, everything he wrote in his mature idiom has the ring of truth, and every note is both absolutely right and profoundly surprising.

Wagner was in conscious reaction against the sentimentality and lassitude of official art. Like Baudelaire (whose admiring letter to the composer after the Parisian performance of *Tannhauser* displays a self-conscious affinity) he saw that the ideal had fled from the world into the citadel of the imagination. Unlike Baudelaire, however, he believed that the ideal could be tempted back, so as to dwell among us (though at considerable public expense). He therefore tried to create a new musical public, one that would not merely see the point of the heroic ideal, but also adopt it. This attempt was already doomed when Wagner first conceived it, and his sacerdotal presumptions have never ceased to alienate those who feel threatened by his message. Hence modern producers, embarrassed by dramas that make a mockery of their way of life, decide in their turn to make a mockery of the dramas. Of course, even today, musicians and singers, responding as they must to the urgency and sincerity of the music, do their best to produce the sounds that Wagner intended. But the action is invariably caricatured, wrapped in inverted commas, and reduced to the dimensions of a television sitcom. Sarcasm and satire run riot on the stage, not because they have anything to prove or say in the shadow of this unsurpassably noble music, but because nobility has become intolerable. The producer strives to distract the audience from Wagner's message, and to mock every heroic gesture, lest the point of the drama should finally come home. As Michael Tanner has argued, in his succinct and penetrating defence of the composer, modern productions attempt to 'domesticate' Wagner, to bring his dramas down from the exalted sphere in which the music places them, to the world of human trivia, usually in order to make a 'political statement' which, being both blatant and banal, succeeds only in cancelling the rich ambiguities of the drama.[1] In contemporary Wagner productions we see exactly what the transition from modernism to the 'post-modern' world involves, namely, the final rejection of high culture as a redemptive force and the ruination of the sacred in its last imagined form.

---

1   Michael Tanner, *Wagner,* Princeton 1996.

Modern producers were anticipated by Nietzsche, for whom the heroic in Wagner is a sham. Wagner, after all, was a disciple of Feuerbach, for whom gods, saints and heroes are nothing but projections into the void of our finite human perfections. Rather than accept Wagner's characters in the terms suggested by the drama we should, Nietzsche advises, translate them 'into reality, into the modern – let us be even crueller – into the bourgeois!' And what then? We find ourselves among the 'metropolitan' problems of Parisian decadents – 'always five steps from the hospital'.[2]

Nietzsche's judgements are seldom fair, and this is no exception. Wagner was concerned to create a *new* kind of heroism, and to offer a new kind of solace to those of us for whom the old heroic way of life is not available. Heroes of the old type are larger-than-life versions of humanity, who live, love and suffer more completely than the rest of us, and who illustrate the possibilities to which man, with divine assistance, may aspire. Wagner's heroes belong to a new type. They exist in a state of exalted solitude, the result of some primeval mistake; but they long either to redeem or be redeemed, through an act of loving sacrifice. Redemption comes when, having found the love which meets their inner need, they will and achieve their own extinction.

Our sympathy for the Wagnerian hero – a sympathy brilliantly 'managed' by the music which propels him – is not the artificial thing that Nietzsche pilloried. It stems from the deepdown recognition that his predicament is ours. Precisely because we live in a morbidly unheroic world – the world of the cynic and the salesman, in which gods and heroes have no place – we are driven to regard our own existence as some kind of mistake. If it is to have a meaning this can come only through a gesture which throws all calculation aside, which recklessly disregards both cost and benefit and, by freely embracing its own absurdity, reconsecrates our lives. In love we aspire to this, and our lives are briefly irradiated by a sense of the transcendent. But

---

2   Friedrich Nietzsche, *The Case of Wagner,* section 9, in Nietzsche, *The Birth of Tragedy* and *The Case of Wagner,* tr. Walter Kaufmann, New York 1967.

love too degenerates into cost and benefit, and comes to seem like just another version of the primal error. Only in those sublime moments when love prepares to sacrifice itself for the beloved – in other words, when it wills its own extinction – do the salesman and the accountant step back into the shadow.

> The awful daring of a moment's surrender
> Which an age of prudence can never retract . . .

T.S. Eliot's words, written out of a later and bleaker experience of loss, capture the enduring influence of Wagner. These moments in and out of time, Wagner implies, are all that we should mean, and all that we can mean, by redemption. This, and this alone, endows our life with meaning, by sanctifying, from our own resources, the two realities – erotic love and death – which were once sanctified by religion.

Of course, few of us live like that – and, from the point of view of the species, the fewer the better. But that is precisely why Wagner's art is so important. For it raises into conscious and dramatic form the one experience that can rescue godless people from triviality. It shows man the redeemer, who re-enchants the world without divine assistance. The proof that this is possible – even if it is a proof that depends on the highest artistic contrivance – clears the psychic space that we require. We live *as if* we could make that final sacrifice, *as if* we could free ourselves, through some absolute and peremptory self-command, from the original mistake – the mistake of existing in a disenchanted world. This 'as if' permeates our daily thoughts and feelings, and reconciles us to each other and the world.

There is another way of seeing what Wagner is getting at. Modern people are living beyond the death of their gods. And this means that they live with an enhanced awareness of their own contingency – of the fact of being, as Heidegger puts it, thrown down in the world without an explanation. And yet, just as much as their forebears, they are social beings, bound to each other by guilt and shame and hesitation. You do not rescue yourself from this predicament by overcoming guilt and shame. For the person without shame – the one who lives beyond judgement, and in the moment alone – can neither love nor be loved.

He lives in a solipsistic void, where there is neither meaning nor joy, but at best only pleasure.

Love can rescue us from this predicament, not by enabling us to escape our guilt, but by putting us in a position where we confront and expiate it. Love of the highest kind is a pilgrimage to a place of purification. And at that place stands Death, guardian of the ultimate mystery. In love our contingency becomes a necessity, and our mortality a kind of eternity – provided only that we accept these things with fullness of heart, wanting to justify the love that we receive, and to give love in return. We may not achieve the highest renunciation which that ideal requires. But by holding it before us we are steadily redeemed from our original failing. Therefore we should live *as if* a heroic love were possible, and *as if* we could renounce our life for the sake of it.

What is meant by the phrase 'as if'? The Kantian philosopher Hans Vaihinger once presented this term as capturing what is distinctive in the human condition – the thing which sets us apart from the rest of nature, in a world of our own devising.[3] We are able, he argued, to look on the world *as if* a certain thought were true, even while keeping open the possibility of its falsehood – as in a hypothesis – or while not fully believing it – as in many aspects of religion – or while not believing it at all, as in a fiction. And by enduing the world with 'useful fictions' we not only increase our power over it, but begin to shape it according to our social and moral needs.

Of course, if you believe that something – a god, say – is *merely* a fiction, then you are unlikely to respond to it with any lively sense of its power. As Wagner saw, however – and saw more deeply than any other modern artist – a myth is not just a fiction, and our engagement with it is never just a game. The myth sets before us in allegorical form a truth about our condition, but a truth which is veiled in mystery. Through the myth we understand both the thing to which we aspire, and the forces which prevent us from attaining it. And we understand these things not theoretically, but by living through them in imagination and sympathy – as the fate of Demeter is lived through by

---

3   Hans Vaihinger, *The Philosophy of 'As If'*, tr. C.K. Ogden, London 1932.

the one who sings the Homeric hymn to her, or as the crucifixion of Christ is lived through by the choir and congregation during the *St. Matthew Passion.*

The myth, through its reenactment, shapes our emotions, encouraging us to live for the higher state to which the god promises to raise us. This is what happens in the Eucharist, and it is part of the reason why the Eucharist must be constantly repeated. We need to rehearse the transition from the fallen to the redeemed state, in order to renew in ourselves the aspiration towards it.[4] The Eucharist, in providing us with a repeated triumph over evil, over death, and over all that drags us down to the animal kingdom, renews our faith in ourselves as creatures destined to another and higher realm. Even with the death of God the Eucharist retains its magic. For, the religious ceremony is now enacted at the mythical level, and another 'as if' arrests us in our mortal divagations. Such is the theme of that strangest and most ineffable of Wagner's operas – the paganly Christian *Parsifal.*

To understand the depth of the Wagnerian 'as if' is to understand the condition of the modern soul. We know that we are animals, parts of the natural order, bound by laws which tie us to the material forces which govern everything. We believe that the gods are our invention, and that death is exactly what it seems. Our world has been disenchanted and our illusions destroyed. At the same time we cannot live as though that were the whole truth of our condition. Even modern people are compelled to praise and blame, love and hate, reward and punish. Even modern people – especially modern people – are aware of the self, as the centre of their being; and even modern people try to connect to other selves around them. We therefore see others *as if* they were free beings, animated by a self or soul, and with a more than worldly destiny. If we abandon that perception, then human relations dwindle into a machine-like parody of themselves, the world is voided of love, duty and desire, and only the body remains – though centre stage, flicking channels on its

---

4   Here is a wonderful subject for speculation, approached with characteristic loquacity by George Steiner, in *Real Presences,* London 1990.

private TV. Modern science has presented us with the 'as ifness' of human freedom; but it could never equip us to live without the belief in it. And this deep and indispensable 'as if' is what Wagner seizes on in his cosmic myths.

The *Ring* cycle shows us people living in an enchanted world – a world in which the gods roam, brimful of interest in humanity, and in which the forces that thwart and abet us are personalised and prayed to. But this enchantment, which sets the gods in Valhalla and laws in the human world, is also a usurpation. The gods spring from our unconscious needs and strivings – they are thrown off by that great explosion of moral energy, whereby the human community first emerges from the natural order and idealises itself in a common culture. They therefore bear the marks of a deeper nature – a nature which is pre-conscious, pre-moral and unfree. Examine them too closely and their credentials dissolve – and how wonderfully Wagner shows this, not only in the character of Wotan, but in the narrative which constantly and continuously deconstructs him, needs no emphasis. Consequently the gods stand in need of us for their redemption. The old hierarchy of theology is reversed. Only through incarnation in a human being, and the enjoyment of a human freedom, the freedom that comes to the contingent and the created, can the divine achieve salvation. But the freedom that we enjoy is conditional on our mortality. Death lies at the heart of the moral community, and love is a relation between dying things. But love is also, in its highest form, a recognition and acceptance of death. Redemption, therefore, for the gods as much as for us, lies in love and in the exalted acceptance of death which love makes possible.

We do not live in that way. But the drama shows us that we could do so. A new world arises whenever humans dare to be free: the enchanted world of higher and lower, good and evil, god and devil: the world of divinity and distinction. That is the world that Wagner shows us, and if he places his dramas always in some mythic and primeval realm, this is in order to emphasise their trans-historical character. Wagner's dramas are symbolic representations of forces and processes that lie deeper than words, and to which we respond with a sympathy that is a deeper and darker version of our sympathy for people. The

Wagnerian drama creates its own religious background, its own awareness of a more than human cosmic order. And this awareness shines through the deeds of god and hero in much the way that it shines through the actions on the Greek tragic stage.

But we should return for a moment to the argument of Chapter 5. Wagner's idea of erotic love is a direct descendent of Romanticism. Love enters the drama from *outside* the home. It is an untamed, undomesticated force, leading to adultery (*Tristan*) or incest (*Die Walküre*). Love proves itself only in opposition to morality, and by desecrating marriage. Children hardly get a look in; when, in the love of Siegmund and Sieglinde, a child results, it is promptly orphaned, and placed in a home which is not a home at all, but a place of servitude and alienation. And that is why love has no fulfilment in this life, and must will its own extinction: all other means of fulfilment have been cut off by love's own transgression.

If therefore we look at Wagner's heroic ideal not from the internal perspective of the dramas, but from the external perspective of the anthropologist, they offer a striking commentary on our situation. In Wagner we see the erotic severed from its normal rite of passage. Faithful love is guaranteed by no institution, no moral status within the community. It is a condition outside society, in which individuals coalesce in the moral void. Children are no part of their intention, and child-bearing is both accidental and intrinsically tragic, resulting in another individual as lost and as alien as its parents. Despite this, love is experienced as a yearning, all-consuming force: the prelude to some transfiguring change. Such a change is marriage, in which the moral status of the lovers is revised upwards, and fidelity given its communal endorsement. Having rejected marriage – the rite of passage into the community – the Wagnerian lover must therefore choose death – the rite of passage out of it. Any other *telos* would merely trivialise his love, bringing it down to the level of the transient, the substitutable, the aesthetic, the level of Don Juan. And, the critic might say, this shows the untenability of Wagner's heroic ideal. Love cannot in reality be treated in this way. Its higher – that is to say, ethical – form is marriage. The destiny of love lies not in the individual but in the tribe: in the process of reproduction which the rite of passage guarantees.

Take away the rite of passage, and all that remains is a transient and Juanesque desire, whose protestations of fidelity are no more than a sentimental disguise. Indeed, does not Wagner show as much, in the drink of forgetfulness which is offered to Siegfried?

Wagner was greatly admired by Baudelaire, the nocturnal poet of the city; but the heroic has no place in Baudelaire's poetry. Nor does Baudelaire try to rescue the ideal through myth and its re-enactment. For Baudelaire, the ideal, the noble, the ethical itself, all belong to a world that has been called away. He was perhaps the first artist to recognise the gulf that had opened, between the real community which the artist observed, and the imagined community invoked by his language. Eliot wrote that 'it is not merely in the use of imagery of common life, not merely in the use of imagery of the sordid life of a great metropolis, but in the elevation of such imagery to the *first intensity* – presenting it as it is, and yet making it represent something more than itself – that Baudelaire has created a mode of release and expression for other men'.[5] But the words 'first intensity' do not say enough – nor does Eliot's somewhat lame parenthesis. The intensity of experience in Baudelaire is of a piece with an evaluation. It comes about because Baudelaire sets the experience within the spiritual context that shows what it means. For Baudelaire retained in the midst of vacillation the robust sense of sin, and of Hell as the punishment for sin.

This 'recognition of the reality of sin,' Eliot writes, 'is a New Life; and the possibility of damnation is so immense a relief in a world of electoral reform, plebiscites, sex reform and dress reform, that damnation itself is an immediate form of salvation – salvation from the ennui of modern life.' But that too is lame. Reforms and plebiscites count for nothing in *Les fleurs du mal* because they make no impact on the relentless observing consciousness. This consciousness is overborne by a sense of loss – not the loss of paradise, but the loss of that loss, the vaporisation of once holy dreams. The ennui of modern life is the sign of a deeper disorder – the dissipation of the community which gave sacraments their meaning.

---

5   *Selected Essays,* London 1932, p. 426.

Baudelaire's imagery is therefore steeped in the Christian symbols, while his verse forms – the sonnet in particular – invoke a lyrical innocence which is in stark contrast to the scenes of dissipation that they portray. Baudelaire's modernism consists in this: that he takes the old verse-forms, with their implicit reference to a community in touch with its God, and sets them in judgement over the experience of a self-consciously modern person, adrift on a boundless sea of evil, and with no consolation and no triumph save the fact of consciousness itself:

> *Un phare ironique, infernal,*
> *Flambeau des grâces sataniques,*
> *Soulagement et gloire uniques,*
> *– La conscience dans le Mal!*

Such is the task of the modern poet: to show consciousness, alive and judging, in a world that will not be judged. Tradition is of the greatest importance to the modern artist, since it defines the perspective from which judgement is sustained. Hence the renewal of tradition is the most modern of artistic motives. This was the theme of Baudelaire's essays on modern painting, in which he demands that the painter, like the poet, be true to the experience of the modern city. *Le peintre de la vie moderne* offers the justification for Manet's realism; but it also shows why tradition matters to the modernist. You cannot paint modern life merely by producing recognisable images of it – for photographs, which are images of modern life, are also *part* of modern life, in need of the very artistic ordering which they fail to provide. You can paint modern life only if you produce your image of it as *painters* do – which means using brush and pigments with the same broad intention as they were used by Titian, Rembrandt or Gainsborough. That is why modern art is so difficult, and why it has proved necessary to be not merely modern but also modernist. The modernist is the one who consciously reshapes the medium, in order that the *old* intentions can be entertained. The salon art of a Bouguereau may *look* in one sense more like a traditional painting than Manet's *Olympia*. But only in the sense that a photograph may look more like a painting. At a deeper level it looks *nothing* like a traditional painting, any more than a mocking imitation of someone's gesture looks like a sincere human gesture. The intention in Bouguereau's painting is of another order from that which we see in a Raphael or a Titian: with Bouguereau we leave the world of the artist for that of the salesman, and Baudelaire's protest against the salons was among the first outspoken acknowledgements of the existence and depravity of kitsch. Manet's intention is of the same kind as Titian's, but working with other human material and another message.

Of course, in *Olympia* and *Le deéjeuner sur l'herbe,* Manet makes knowing reference to the tradition, and in particular to Titian and Giorgione. But this is not merely in order to advertise his new perspective or to make ironical play with vanished feelings. It is for the very reason that Baudelaire made use of the sonnet, or Schoenberg of the classical forms: in order to show the proximity of his intentions to those which had been central to the art of the past. And here it is worth noting that the self-conscious attempt to be part of a tradition – even the concept of tradition itself – is a modern phenomenon. Artists who are immersed in a tradition have little consciousness of the fact. They create by instinct what later generations must re-create by connoisseurship. It is an accident of modern life that Manet should be familiar with the paintings of Titian. And the obsessive quoting of the art of the past that we find in Picasso or Bacon would have been inconceivable in other ages, not only because of the shortage of information, but because only a modernist would have seen the point of it. Only a modernist has the problem of staying true to an artistic enterprise which must be re-made if it is to exist at all. Only a modernist is concerned to *situate* himself and his art in history. Modernism is essentially a view from outside.

But let us return to literature, since it is in literature that modern life first defined itself. In Baudelaire we find the most important project of modernism: the attempt to revive the spirit by offending it. The fall into sensuality, the opium-pillowed lassitude, the open wound of sex and the alcoholic haze that both obscures despair and heightens it – all these are evoked in exquisite language, so as to become forms of moral suffering, *ordeals* of the spirit that paradoxically prove through its degradation that the spirit belongs elsewhere. (See, for example, the verse

preface to *Les fleurs du Mal,* and the sonnet entitled 'Recueille-
ment'.) The project was taken up by Baudelaire's immediate suc-
cessors – by no one more ferociously than Rimbaud – and later
by T.S. Eliot, the first true modernist in English literature. *The
Waste Land* effects a remarkable synthesis: on the one hand
Baudelaire's experience of the city as a spiritual ordeal, giving
proof of our higher nature by depicting its ruin. (The verse preface to *Les Fleurs du mal* is significantly quoted.) On the other
hand, the self-conscious appeal to myth, which outlines the original community, the divinely ordained order and lost Edenic innocence, from which all our wanderings and grievings decline.
The ruling influences in this second enterprise are two: anthropology, for its vision of myth as the flowering of a common culture, and Wagner, for his attempt to use myth as part of the
redeeming alchemy of art. At each point in Eliot's invocation of
modern London we find two artistic givens – the alienated observer and, in the soul of that observer, the echoing vault of a
vanished religious culture, in which the fragments of experience
seek their completion in myth. The vault echoes with the words
of poets: Dante, Shakespeare, Verlaine, Nerval, Wagner. Its
walls are crowded with symbols, from the legend of the grail,
from Christianity, and from other cults of the 'dying god'. These
echoes and symbols are there not to establish Eliot's place in the
high culture of Europe, but to create, in imagination, an ideal
common culture – a deep-down collective experience which will
supply the meaning which is absent from the fragments. The anthropological vision of Christianity as a vegetation cult is internalised. The ruined soulscape of the modern city calls for the
refreshing rain of Christ's passion. And the alienated observer is
both Christ and the pilgrim seeking him – the soul for whom suffering is also a mystical redemption.

What explains the extraordinary impact of this poem – its
claim to be a founding document of modern English literature?
The answer is surely obvious. In *The Waste Land* our high culture at last comes clean: the myths and legends that had fed the
Arthurian twilight, and thereby sentimentalised and falsified
modern life, are, in this poem, subjected to anthropological dis-
section, and returned to their grave. The poem openly confesses

to its loss. High culture hurts because it is bereft. For a century it has denied the death of the common culture that gave sense to it; now it can acknowledge its loss. What Freud called 'the work of mourning' has, in this poem, begun. The poem invokes the dying god, and the communal emotions which he symbolised, while showing the world as it is when the god withdraws from it – when the god dies for the last time, and the miraculous rebirth no longer happens. The theme had already been explored by Wagner in *Parsifal,* a work whose influence is everywhere apparent in Eliot's poem. But the redemption that is offered – some might say contrived – by Wagner, is only mourned by Eliot, as a thing irretrievably lost.

The Waste Land both acknowledges the death of God and also implies that God's death can never be acknowledged, since to confront this supreme bereavement is to enter a condition of penitential suffering akin to prayer. The desolation of the god-forsaken city is proof of that higher world from which the soul descends. This vision of a higher world is there, of course, in Tennyson and Rossetti, and it pervades the sad, thin literature of the Edwardians and Georgians. But in their stilted diction and reproduction-antique style the vision becomes a lie. It constitutes a denial of modern life, of the machine, of the implacable city, and of the society of strangers. By sentimentalising the human soul, the late Romantics shift the focus of emotion; the soul is etherealised, advertised, remade as a charming simulacrum and so auctioned off.

In Eliot the modern experience finds artistic form, without losing its reference to a redeemed and higher life. Eliot's modernism is also a realism – an avoidance of sentimentality. For, as Eliot made wonderfully clear in his critical essays, sentimentality causes us not merely to write in clichés, but to *feel* in clichés too, lest we be troubled by the truth of our condition. The task of the artistic modernist, as Eliot later expressed it, borrowing from Mallarmé, is 'to purify the dialect of the tribe': that is, to find the words, rhythms, and artistic forms that would make contact again with our experience – not my experience or yours, but *our* experience – the experience that unites us as living here and now.

Eliot's artistic modernism was the start of a spiritual quest, which ended only when he embraced the Christian religion, in the eccentric and localised form defined by the doctrine and liturgy of the Anglican church. For Nietzsche, the crisis of modernity had come about because of the loss of the Christian faith. At the same time, as Nietzsche, Wagner and Baudelaire all acknowledged, it is not possible for mankind really to live without faith; and for those who have inherited the habits and concepts of a Christian culture, that faith must be Christianity. Take away the faith, and you do not take away a body of doctrine only; nor do you leave a clear uncluttered landscape in which man is at last visible for what he is. You take away the power to perceive other and more important *truths* – truths about our condition which cannot, without the support of faith, be confronted. (For example, the truth of our mortality, which is not simply a scientific fact, to be added to our store of knowledge, but a pervasive *experience,* which runs through all things and changes the aspect of the world.)

The solution which Nietzsche impetuously embraced in this quandary was to deny the sovereignty of truth altogether – to hold that 'there are no truths', and to build a philosophy of life on the ruins of both science and religion, in the name of a purely aesthetic ideal. This response is doomed to failure; for the aesthetic is rooted in the religious and provides no emotional fruit when severed from its root. Eliot saw this; but the paradox remains for Eliot too. The truths that mattered to Eliot are truths of *feeling,* truths about the *weight* of human life, and the reality of human attachments. Science does not make these truths more easily perceivable: on the contrary, it prompts us to see our situation from outside, to consider human emotion as we might consider the mating habits of curious insects, and so clouds the psyche with fantasies. The result is a corruption of the very language of feeling, a decline from sensibility to sentimentality, and a veiling of the human world. The paradox is this: the falsehoods of religious faith reveal the truths that matter. The truths of science conceal the human reality. Eliot's solution to the paradox was compelled by the path that he had taken to its discovery – the path of poetry, with its agonising examples of poets whose precision, perception and sincerity were the gifts of doctrine. The solution was to embrace the Christian faith, not, as Tertullian did, *because* of the paradox, but rather in spite of it.

For Eliot conversion was a gesture of belonging, an imaginative homecoming whereby he united himself with an historical common culture. This culture was, for Eliot, at once local and placeless, present and timeless, the possession of a community sanctified by history, and transcending history through prayer. To pass on a culture we must also inherit it, and inheritance is an active and arduous process, no longer granted automatically as it is granted to the tribesman. We must listen to the voices of the dead, and capture their meaning in those elusive moments when 'History is now and England'. Only in a religious community are such moments part of everyday life. For us, in the modern world, religion and culture are both to be *gained* through a work of sacrifice. But it is a sacrifice on which redemption of the poet depends. Hence, by an extraordinary route, the modernist poet becomes the traditionalist priest: the stylistic task of the one coalesces with the spiritual task of the other. The renewal of the artistic tradition is also a re-affirmation of orthodoxy.

Eliot was not alone in seeing the problem of the modern artist in theological terms. The same idea – that the reinvention of the artistic tradition and the rediscovery of the religious community are one and the same spiritual exercise – animates the work of Arnold Schoenberg, and is dramatised in his unfinished opera, *Moses and Aaron* (which breaks off, however, with a bleak recognition of the hopelessness of the task that the artist-priest has set himself). Nor is this religious emphasis surprising. The question for the modernist is this: can you rediscover the ethical vision in the midst of modern life, without some equivalent of faith – some self-guaranteeing vision of the community and its gods? We should not be surprised to find that so many modernists have been religious traditionalists: Stravinsky, for example, Messiaen, Britten, Matisse and Henry Moore. Modern artists may withdraw from or lose their religious convictions. But often they lose their modernism too, like Richard Strauss or Ralph Vaughan Williams (who nevertheless made some of the last great additions to the Anglican hymnal). Failing that, they may try to invent a new and subjective religion, through which to invoke a kind of one-ness with the collective unconscious that is not available in life as it is lived. (Rilke, for example, Lawrence, and the Joyce of *Finnegans Wake.)* They may offer a meditation on God's absence, in which the human subject disintegrates for lack of communal endorsement, as in the novels and plays of Beckett. In all these endeavours the religious need reaches through the aesthetic and endows it with its urgency and force.

Modernists who have found themselves unable to subscribe to their ancestral religion have sometimes, like Eliot in *The Waste Land,* reconstructed the religious context through an anthropologist's eye: witness Picasso's early fascination with the art of Africa, through which he rescued himself, just in time, from the sentimentality of his 'Blue' period. Or witness Stravinsky in *The Rite of Spring,* Yeats in his Celtic Twilight, Janáček, Vaughan Williams and Bartók, as they scoured the countryside for natural music, sung simply and sincerely by people not yet discovered by the travelling salesman. Whether or not they were aware of it, these artists were engaged in a spiritual pilgrimage, searching for the traces left by forgotten tribes. Nothing is more striking than the collapse of the modernist project when the religious motive dies. The result is the sterile mass- production of Picasso in his later years, or the desiccated perfectionism of Boulez, whose *Marteau sans maître* survives in the archive, the last pressed flower in the book of modernism, a memento mori which we study from time to time and then wistfully return to its grave.

Modernists who have not taken Eliot's path (for it is an overgrown path, and leads only to abandoned ruins) have, as a rule, taken Wagner's, weaving modern life into a mythic version of itself, in which those very things which most disturb us are somehow re-shaped as our redemption. The Wagnerian 'as if' dominates the modernist novel, from Joyce to Patrick White, and from Mann to Nabokov. The transfiguration of the commonplace, to borrow Arthur Danto's trenchant phrase, is also the Eucharist of modern art.

We should always revere the modernist heroes. But the world has changed, and their agenda cannot be ours. As my examples show, modernism involves too great a divorce between the high culture of its adepts, and the religious feelings to which it makes appeal. Standing vigil at the grave of the old religion, modernism maintains its unearthly dignity for year after year.

But the grave is less and less visited, and the display looks more and more redundant and absurd. Without the religious motive, and the ingrained reverence towards a sacred text, the trouble demanded by high culture seems an excessive price to pay for its dubious privilege. And there arises what has become, for teachers of the humanities, the most pressing of moral dilemmas. Do we attempt to impart our culture to the young, knowing that we can do so only by requiring efforts which they themselves may see as wasted? Or do we leave them to their own devices, and allow the culture which shaped us, and which provides our lasting images of value, to die? These questions define the post-modern predicament.

8
Avant-garde and Kitsch

The first effect of modernism was to make high-culture difficult: to surround beauty with a wall of erudition. The hidden purpose was twofold: to protect art against popular entertainment, and to create a new barrier, a new obstacle to membership, and a new rite of passage to the adult and illuminated sphere. To those whom modernism excluded, the movement seemed like a betrayal of the past. Tonality and tunefulness in music; the human image in painting; the pleasing dignity of metre and rhyme – even the homely comfort of a story well told – all these ways in which art had opened its arms to normal humanity were suddenly rejected, like a false embrace. To the modernists, however, the past was betrayed not be modernism but by popular culture. Tonal harmonies had been corrupted and banalised by popular music; figurative painting had been trumped by photography; rhyme and metre had become the stuff of Christmas cards, and the stories had been too often told. Everything out there, in the world of naïve and unthinking people, was kitsch. Modernism was not an assault on the artistic tradition, but an attempt to rescue it. Such was the surprising thought expressed by Eliot and Schoenberg, and their eloquence transformed the high culture of Europe.[1]

Popular culture is too complex a phenomenon to be summarily dismissed – as it was dismissed, for example, by Schoenberg's great champion, Theodor Adorno.[2] In this chapter

---

1   See T.S. Eliot, 'Tradition and the Individual Talent', in *The Sacred Wood,* London 1920, and A. Schoenberg, *Harmonielehre,* 3rd edition, Vienna 1932, p. 288f, the argument of which is summarised in R. Scruton, *The Aesthetics of Music,* Oxford 1997, pp 285–294.

2   For example in *The Philosophy of Modern Music,* tr. A.G. Mitchell and W.V. Blomster, New York 1973 – a book relent-

and the two that follow I shall therefore isolate certain elements in popular culture, and try to put them in their social and religious context. When faith is no longer a given, but either a precarious survival or a hard-won personal achievement, then the need for religion breaks out in novel forms, some acknowledging their religious basis, like the New Age spasms which briefly shake the young, some overtly denying it, as in the now extinct, or at any rate dormant, volcanoes of fascism and communism. But each represents a surge of visceral collective feeling, as people lose themselves in a cause that will swamp the psyche and drown the grief of solitude. These substitute religions are marked by the thing which the modernists deplored – sentimentality, by which I mean the desire for the glory of some heroic or transfiguring passion, without the cost of feeling it. Inevitably, the attempt to express them in artistic forms will go the way of the official art of communist and fascist societies: it will remain on the level of kitsch, like socialist realism or the Nuremberg rallies. Indeed kitsch, as I see it, is a religious phenomenon – an attempt to disguise the loss of faith, by filling the world with fake emotions, fake morality and fake aesthetic values.

The loss of faith which has infected popular culture has infected modernism too. Without the background of a remembered faith, modernism loses its conviction: it becomes routinised. For a long time now it has been assumed that there can be no authentic creation in the sphere of high art which is not in some way a 'challenge' to the ordinary public. Art must give offence, stepping out of the future fully armed against the bourgeois taste for kitsch and cliché. But the result of this is that offence becomes a cliché. If the public has become so immune to shock that only a dead shark in formaldehyde will awaken a brief spasm of outrage, then the artist must produce a dead shark in formaldehyde – this, at least, is an authentic gesture. In place of Harold Rosenberg's 'tradition of the new', we have the 'cliché of the unexpected'. This is not the originality sought with such care and pain by the modernists, but a repetition of the would-be unrepeatable.

To understand the forms of post-modern culture we should

---

lessly criticised in R. Scruton, *op. cit.*

examine three contemporary phenomena: the modernist establishment, kitsch and pop. In a curious way these things belong together; they are the great forms that lie beached on the shore of human leisure as high culture recedes.

The great modernists were catholic, open-minded and acutely aware of the need to build bridges to the public whose expectations they disturbed. They ended, like Eliot, Picasso, Moore and Stravinsky, by being genuinely loved by those who cared for the traditional high culture. But they began by being difficult – *intentionally* difficult, in order that an effective bulwark should exist between the high ground of art and the swamp of popular sentiment. And because they were difficult, there grew around the modernists a class of critics and impresarios, who offered initiation into the modernist cult. This impresario class began to promote the incomprehensible and the outrageous as a matter of course, lest the public should regard its services as redundant. It owes much to state patronage, which is now the principal source of funding for high culture; it shares in the serene unanswerability of all bureaucracies with power to reward the 'experts' appointed to oversee them. And it fosters a new kind of personality, animated by the snobbery of a vanishing era, and determined to move with the times, while understanding less and less what the times might actually be. To convince himself that he is a true progressive, who rides in the vanguard of history, the new impresario surrounds himself with others of his kind, promoting them to all committees which are relevant to his status, and expecting to be promoted in his turn. Thus arises the modernist establishment, which has dominated the official culture of Europe for the last three decades, and which shows no sign of loosening its grip.

Once institutionalised, modernism loses its character as an attempt to recover the tradition, and becomes instead a game, of no greater significance than the surrounding popular culture, and distinguished only by the erudite nature of the pain involved in enduring it. The presence of important financial incentives hastened the death of traditional painting, by devaluing the fund of artistic knowledge and encouraging minor talents to dispense with the humility which might otherwise have caused them to study and emulate the masters. Thus abstract painting embarked on an entirely new course – and this new course could fairly be called 'post-modernist', in that it follows in the footsteps of modernism, while repudiating the spiritual enterprise that gave modernism its rationale.

For Mondrian, Nicholson and Klee abstract art was just that: an art of abstraction. An artist like Ben Nicholson abstracted the visual essence from a figurative design, so as to bring out the secret harmony of things that inhabit our space. He was going one stage further down the path marked out for us by Cézanne – the path which leads away from fleeting appearances to appearances of another, deeper and more durable kind, in which spiritual order is discovered in the simplest things, by refining away the dross of present perception. Abstraction came about through the ever-narrowing focus of the aesthetic gaze.

The post-modern offshoots of abstract art may seem to be engaged in the same artistic project; but the appearance is, it seems to me, deceptive. Post-modern abstraction is really *construction,* in which abstract elements are combined *ab initio,* and without reference to the natural forms and perceptions which might first have endowed them with a meaning. The shapes, lines and colours may never have been bathed, for the painter, in the light of reality. Their purpose is not to capture and make permanent the hidden structure of appearances, but to glorify the sovereign role of the artist, who shifts and arranges them as would a child playing with coloured blocks. Constructionism is a ploy, which, by making the artist into the creator of his world, cuts off any external judgement, any comparison with things as they are. The world of the constructivist is no larger than the psyche of the person who makes it. The result has been a sudden narrowing of the artistic intention, and a launching of post-modern art towards bombast and doodling by turns.[3]

This triumph of the construct over the abstract is one part of the routinisation of modernism, and its conversion into the

---

3   Readers will have their own examples. For doodles try Cy Twombly; for bombast Richard Serra or Julian Schnabel. The cultural impact of abstract art in America is a subject for the satirist, effectively undertaken by Tom Wolfe in *The Painted Word,* and, with dead-pan penetration, by William Boyd, in *Nat Tate: American Artist.*

official style of an 'avant-garde establishment'. The construct has art and not life as its model; it is built according to a system, and its very originality is contained in the rules for its production. It triggers the quick response of the establishment critic, who knows that he will make no mistake by praising it, for the very reason that no-one, not even the artist, will understand why he does so, and therefore no-one will be in a position to doubt his taste.

To the same cause may be attributed the invasive nature of post-modern art, its tendency to colonise every available inch of floor, wall or ceiling, in order to drive out from our perceptions all that is not art, all that is merely decorative, homely and unassuming. This tendency leads inevitably to the 'installation', in which art extinguishes competition, and takes up residence at the very point where reality should be. In the installation art becomes sovereign, and in consequence loses its nature as art.

When the works of the impressionists sought their public, they came sealed in baroque and Renaissance frames, whose lively designs and inescapable symmetries confined the paintings to a space of their own, maintaining their simultaneous identities, on the one hand as furniture, on the other hand as vistas into imaginary worlds. There was a tact, a modesty and a good nature about this, which gave confidence to the public and a focus to the artistic intention. A painting in a frame does not have a boundary: it is *cut off* by the frame, creating the illusion of a world glimpsed as from a window. You enter the painting by passing through the frame; the day-to-day reality remains uncontaminated by the work of art, just as the work of art is insulated from reality. The frame is there to create an imaginative space that stands in no spatial relation to the world of the observer. (It is above all its spatiality – the fact that it occupies some part of our space – that distinguishes the sculpted from the painted image.)

Constructionist paintings seldom come with frames; indeed, they tend to be unframeable, defying the symmetries that would enable us to confine them. They are in a certain manner imperious, often recognising no limit to their sovereignty over their surroundings. The place where they stand becomes an 'exhibition space', and their presence in a room turns it from a private home to a public gallery. They do not occur in the background of human life; rather, human life creeps around them, distracted by their presence, and unsure of the nature and extent of the reverence which is due to them. Their presence is an *official* presence, and their very dullness serves to emphasise their message, which is that art is no longer a reflection on human life but a mechanism for excluding it.

The routinisation of the modernist gesture should be set in its historical context – which is that of kitsch and kitschophobia. If we look back to the pre-history of modernism we find occasional lapses into sentimentality – we plainly observe it, for example, in Murillo, Guido Reni or Greuze. We also discover art which is mechanical and cliché-ridden – like much of Telemann and Vivaldi. But we find nothing that could be described without a sense of strain as kitsch – not even Vivaldi's *Seasons*. The artless art of primitive people; the art of the medieval stone-masons and stained-glass makers; the art of the Minnesingers and of the Eddas and Sagas – all these are naïve and devoid of high pretensions. Yet none is kitsch, nor could it be. They never prompt that half-physical revulsion which is our spontaneous tribute to kitsch in all its forms.

At some point during the Enlightenment all that changed. And today the mere contact of a primitive culture with Western civilisation is sufficient to transmit the disease, rather as primitive people were once rescued from their darkness by our colonial adventurers and missionaries, only to die at once from smallpox or TB. Much African art today is kitsch; a century ago none of it was.

Here it is important to make a crucial distinction, without which the history of modern culture cannot be properly understood: that between the aesthetic object and the advert.

To sell a product, you must inform the world of its existence. For this purpose the message must be undemanding and accessible. But advertising has acquired a life of its own; it acts not on the customer's beliefs but on his desires, by offering a fantasy form of membership. Advertised goods exist in two worlds – one real, the other imaginary. And the second attracts the frustrated emotions which the real world cannot satisfy.

The advert is similar to the aesthetic object, but crucially different in this: that it must neutralise the critical faculty, and arrest the process whereby the actual is compared with its ideal and the ideal with the actual. The work of art endows its subject with intrinsic value, and therefore upholds the distinction between things with a value and things with a price. The advert erodes that distinction; it creates a fantasy world in which value can be purchased, so that price and value are one and the same. The advert is analogous to Freud's 'dream-work' – an exercise in wish-fulfilment. But by fulfilling the wish in fantasy, it creates the wish in fact.

Faith exalts the human heart, by removing it from the market-place, making it sacred and unexchangeable. Under the jurisdiction of religion our deeper feelings are sacralised, so as to become raw material for the ethical life: the life lived in judgement. When faith declines, however, the sacred is unprotected from marauders; the heart can be captured and put on sale. When this happens the human heart becomes kitsch. The clichéd kiss, the doe-eyed smile, the Christmas-card sentiments advertise what cannot be advertised without ceasing to be. They therefore commit the salesman to nothing; they can be bought and sold without emotional hardship, since the emotion, being a fantasy product, no longer exists in its committed and judgement-bearing form.

Much of our present cultural situation can be seen as a response to this remarkable phenomenon – never, I think, encountered before in history (although noticed in other terms by Théophile Gautier, in his preface to Baudelaire's *Fleurs du mal*). Kitsch reflects our spiritual waywardness, and our failure, not merely to *value* the human spirit, but to perform those sacrificial acts which *create* it. Nor is kitsch a purely aesthetic disease. Every ceremony, every ritual, every public display of emotion can be kitsched – and inevitably will be kitsched, unless controlled by some severe critical discipline, such as Arnold and his followers have conceived to be the social role of high culture. (Think of the Disneyland versions of monarchical and state occasions which are rapidly replacing the old stately forms.) In one of the few existing studies of the phenomenon the novelist Hermann Broch suggests that we speak not of kitsch art or culture, but of the 'Kitschmensch' – the kitschified human type – who lives in this culture and also requires it.[4] This is one reason why you might doubt that Eliot's pilgrimage is still available. It is surely impossible to flee from kitsch by taking refuge in religion, when religion itself is kitsch. The 'modernisation' of the Roman Catholic Mass and the Anglican Prayer Book were really a 'kitschification': and attempts at liturgical art are now poxed all over with the same disease. The day-to-day services of the Christian churches are embarrassing reminders of the fact that religion is losing its sublime godwardness, and turning instead towards the world of mass production. And surely Eliot was right to imply that we cannot overcome kitsch through art alone: the recovery of the tradition is also a reorganisation of our lives, and involves a spiritual as well as an aesthetic transformation.

For a long time the official art of the modernist bureaucracy derived its credentials from kitschophobia. The critic Clement Greenberg famously presented the task of the contemporary artist in a stark dilemma: avant-garde or kitsch, and then did his best to ensure a stampede towards 'abstract expressionism', as having the sole title to critical acclaim.[5] Since Greenberg's essay was published, figurative painting (as in John Wonnacott and David Inshaw), tonal music (as in David Del Tredici or Robert Simpson), and classical architecture (as in Quinlan Terry or Léon Krier) have been regarded with suspicion: they seem manifestly to ignore the kitsch-strewn path onto which the artist strays, once he puts aside the lamp of rectitude that was lit for us by Baudelaire and Manet. Of course, the bureaucracy says, you can turn back to figurative painting, to tonality, to classicism – but you will only be *imitating* these things, never actually *doing* them. You can *make* the old gestures; but you cannot seriously *mean* them. And if you make them nonetheless the result will be kitsch – standard, cut-price goods, produced without effort and consumed without thought.

However self-serving that reaction may be, all cultivated people feel the force of it. In art there comes a point where a

---

4   'Einigen Bemerkungen zum Problem des Kitsches', in *Dichten und Erkennen,* Frankfurt 1976.

5   'Avant-garde and Kitsch', *Partisan Review* 1939, reprinted in Clement Greenberg, *Art and Culture,* New York 1961.

style, a form, an idiom, or a vocabulary can no longer be used without producing kitsch. Fear of kitsch led to the routinisation of modernism. By posing as a modernist, the artist gives an easily perceivable sign of his authenticity. But the result is cliché of another kind, and a loss of genuine public interest. Patronage (much of it from the state) keeps the modernist bureaucracy in business; but its position as the censor of modern culture is inherently unsustainable.

This is one reason for the emergence of a wholly new artistic enterprise, which some call 'postmodernism' but which might better be described as 'pre-emptive kitsch'. Having recognised that modernist severity is no longer acceptable – for modernism begins to seem like the same old thing, and therefore as not modern at all – artists began not to shun kitsch but to embrace it, in the manner of Andy Warhol, Alan Jones and Jeff Koons. The worst thing is to be unwittingly guilty of producing kitsch; far better to produce kitsch deliberately, for then it is not kitsch at all but a kind of sophisticated parody. (The intention to produce *real* kitsch is an impossible intention, like the intention to act unintentionally.) Pre-emptive kitsch sets quotation marks around actual kitsch, and hopes thereby to save its artistic credentials. The dilemma is not: kitsch or avant-garde, but: kitsch or 'kitsch' – kitsch insolently laughing at itself.

In the place of modernist severity, therefore, there comes a kind of institutionalised flippancy. Public galleries and big collections fill with the pre-digested clutter of modern life, brash items of salesmanship which pass their sell-by date the moment they go on permanent display. Art as we knew it required knowledge, competence, discipline and study, all of which were effective reminders of the adult world. Pre-emptive kitsch, by contrast, delights in the tacky, the ready-made, and the cut-out, using forms, colours and images which both legitimise ignorance and also laugh at it, effectively silencing the adult voice. Such art eschews subtlety, allusion and implication, and in place of imagined ideals in gilded frames it offers real junk in quotation marks. It is indistinguishable in the end from advertising – with the sole qualification that it has no product to sell except itself. In this connection it is worth quoting an interview given by Damien Hirst, in the September 1997 issue of *Dazed and Confused*.

'When I think about it,' Hirst says, 'my whole understanding of art has been based on images. I spent more time in the art library and watching TV than ever I did in galleries. I used to go into the art library and say to myself: "I wish I could be like these guys; these are the guys, these are the dons." Sitting there, looking at 5x4 images of paintings, that was the world that I grew up in. At the same time, though, I spent a hell of a lot of time talking about commercials when I was at art school, conversations like, "My God, did you see the Coalite advert where the dog kisses the cat and then the cat kisses the mouse? Fantastic!" That's the one that Tony Kaye did a few years back where the theme tune plays [singing] "Will you still love me tomorrow?" Just a brilliant advert. I didn't realise at the time, but that was where the real art was coming from – the rest of it was in the art library going: "Shit, I wish I could understand all this stuff".'

That is the authentic voice of the post-modern culture – not quite discarding the high culture of our civilisation, but reluctant to make the effort to embrace it. Things have moved on since then, partly under the influence of Hirst himself, and the advert, the comic and the photographic image have now de-throned the painted image and all that it stood for. It is a law of human nature, confirmed by social revolutions throughout modern history, that old authorities, when they fall from their eminence, are instantly trampled on before being kicked aside. We should not be surprised, therefore, to discover that sacrilege and blasphemy have been such important ingredients in 'Young British Art'. Modernism was a last-ditch attempt to save the religious view of man; pre-emptive kitsch asserts its sovereign rights by scorning all religion, all attempts to rescue the 'higher' vision of our nature, and by showing every human hope as kitsch of another kind.

But here we should look again at those post-modernist quotation marks. Maybe, after all, they are what they seem: not a sign of sophistication, but a sign of pretence. Quotation marks are one thing when localised and confined. But they are another thing when generalised, so as to imprison everything we say. For then they make no contrast and lose their ironical force. Generalised inverted commas neither assert nor deny what they contain, but merely present it. The result is not art but 'art' –

pretend art, which bears the same relation to the artistic tradition as a doll bears to human beings.

And the sentiments conveyed by this 'art' are similar: elaborate fakes, as remote from real emotion as the kitsch which they pretend to satirise. The advertising techniques automatically turn emotional expression into kitsch. Hence the inverted commas neutralise and discard the only effect that postmodernist 'art' could ever accomplish. Pre-emptive kitsch offers fake emotion, and at the same time a fake satire of the thing it offers. The artist pretends to take himself seriously, the critics pretend to judge his product and the modernist establishment pretends to promote it. At the end of all this pretence, someone who cannot perceive the difference between advertisement and art decides that he should buy it. Only at this point does the chain of pretence come to an end, and the real value of postmodernist art reveal itself – namely, its value in exchange. Even at this point, however, the pretence is important. For the purchaser must believe that what he buys is real art, and therefore intrinsically valuable, a bargain at any price. Otherwise the price would reflect the obvious fact that anybody – even the purchaser – could have faked such a product.[6]

This chapter has traced the history of visual art since modernism. The modernists tried to rescue high art from the sea of fake emotion; but the new barriers with which they marked off the higher life were captured by a priesthood of impresarios; modernism was thereafter routinised and deprived of its point. Artists ceased to defend themselves from kitsch, and adopted it instead, in a pre-emptive form. The result might be called cultural 'pre-emptiness': not a new form of art, but an elaborate pretence at art, a pretence at appreciation, and a pretence at criticism. And this story shows something about our cultural situation. You will not understand modern high culture, it seems to me, if you do not see that much of it – perhaps the major part of it – is a pretence.

---

6   Perhaps it is unnecessary to refer at this point to the collection of Charles Saatchi, recently seen in New York.

9
Surface and Surfeit

There is a great divide between the high culture of modern civilisation and the popular culture upon which it broods. Some identify kitsch as a cause of this divide, others as the effect of it. Either way it is clear that modern artists have feared contamination from devices which are mechanical, trite and incapable of being used to convey a serious view of life, and that such devices are nevertheless popular, since they require no effort from their intended public. Modernism is a defence against banality: a way of insisting that the audience think.

Technology has also contributed to the divide between high and popular culture. The market can now be flooded at a moment's notice with products that are both easy to grasp and impossible to ignore. The very fact that we can speak of a cultural 'market' testifies to the change undergone by the artistic enterprise in 'the age of mechanical reproduction', as Walter Benjamin described it. High culture is an activity in which the producer is sovereign; pop culture, like every market, shows the sovereignty of the consumer.

The invention of the cinema was seen as both a threat, and an opportunity. Some looked forward to a new era of democratic art, of dramas addressed to the whole population, using images that were appealing and exciting even to those who had never read a book. Others feared that this democratic art would subvert the aims of high culture, by awakening the easy-going fantasies which destroy the mental discipline on which art depends.

To understand the cinema we must first understand photography, which is its medium. Painting was shocked into self-consciousness by the invention of photography, though not, perhaps, into true self-knowledge. If the purpose of painting is to copy appearances and to place a frame around the world then, it was argued, photography can do this just as well or better. So the true purpose of painting must be something else – the recording of a sensory impression (impressionism) or the 'expression' of emotion ('abstract expressionism'). In either case, mere 'representation' – which is the prerogative of photography – is not the ultimate goal.

Such arguments were put forward by way of saving the art of painting from the threat of the camera, and re-launching it on its path to higher things. Two philosophers – the Italian Benedetto Croce and the Englishman R.G. Collingwood – bolstered the defence of painting by giving theories of representation and expression which made expression the true aim of art, and representation at best the means to it. Photography, they suggested, is confined by its nature to the task of representation: it shows the world, but expresses nothing. It is the visual equivalent of journalism, pampering the appetite for knowledge, while destroying, through its expressive incompetence, the act of communication – the resonance of each to each – upon which art depends.

The argument is wrong: not because photography is an art on a par with painting, but because photography does not represent anything at all. It may be an art, but if so, it is not an art of depiction.

Representation occurs in painting; it also occurs in literature, where there is no question of copying the way things appear. Literature and painting represent things, not by copying them, but by expressing thoughts about them. The word 'about' is one of the most difficult in the language. It seems to denote a relation – between thought and its subject matter. But we can think and speak about non-existent things, and what could be meant by a relation between objects, one of which does not exist? Painting is exactly analogous to thought and speech. If you paint a subject, it does not follow that the subject exists, nor, if it does exist, that it is as you paint it to be. And your painting can be of a man, even when there is no particular man of which it is a painting. In the jargon of philosophy: the relation between a painting and its subject is an intentional, not a material, relation.

A photograph is caused by its subject, and causality is a material relation. Hence the subject of the photograph must exist, and if a photograph is of a man, there is some particular man of whom it is a photograph. Furthermore, the photograph will always show the subject, within limits, as it really appeared from a certain angle: and this, indeed is the root of our interest in photography. Of course, the appearance may be deceptive, but the deception lies in the thing photographed, and not in the process of recording it.

Hence, photographs are incapable of displaying things that are unreal. I may take a photograph of a nude and call it Venus. The result, however, is not a photograph of Venus: still less a photographic representation of her. It is a photograph of a representation of Venus: the representational act, the act which establishes the 'intentional relation' with Venus, was completed before the photograph was taken. Photographic fictions are really photographs of fictions; the camera itself is without imagination. Interest in a photograph – even in the arty photographs of a Robinson or a Lartigue – is always interest in the thing photographed, whose existence can never be in doubt. Interest in a painting is in the presentation of a subject, which exists as a rule only in the act of presentation. That is why there is no room, in the true art of painting, for vulgar curiosity, or for those vicarious emotions which hunger for what is distant, disengaged but real.

By its very nature photography can 'depict' things only by resembling them. It is only because photographs look like their subjects that we were ever tempted to compare them with paintings in the first place. In looking at a photograph, therefore, we know that we see something which actually occurred, as it occurred. This fact dominates our response to the picture, which becomes in consequence transparent to its subject. If the picture holds our interest, it is because we are interested in the thing 'shown within'. The beauty of a photograph is seen as a beauty in its subject, and if the photograph is sad, it is because the subject is sad. Consider, for example, Roman Vishniac's superb records of the Central European ghettoes between the wars. The emotional density here belongs not to the picture but to the thing displayed, and is entirely dependent upon our knowledge that this is how things were. Hence there cannot be a photograph of a martyrdom which is other than horrifying. To take an aesthetic interest in a photograph of martyrdom is to sink into moral corruption – the corruption involved in looking aesthetically upon the sufferings of real people. By contrast, a painting of a martyrdom may be serene, as is Mantegna's great crucifixion in the Louvre. The painting, because it tells a story, can create the distance between itself and its subject matter which is necessary for aesthetic judgement. The photograph is unable to do this, since it lacks the technique whereby the subject and its mode of presentation could be held apart.

Well, you might say, why not invent that technique? Suppose that we do so. Suppose that we try to make our photographs so that it no longer matters whether their subjects exist, or whether they look like the things depicted. In such a circumstance, we begin to separate our interest in the picture from our interest in the thing displayed: perhaps we can now take an aesthetic attitude to the one which is not also an aesthetic attitude to the other; perhaps medium and content have at last been pulled apart.

Unfortunately, there is no way of determining in advance which detail is relevant to an aesthetic interest: every detail can and ought to play its part. At the same time, the causal process of which the photographer is victim puts almost every detail outside his control. Even if he does intentionally arrange the folds of his subject's dress and meticulously construct, as studio photographers once used to do, the appropriate scenario, that would still hardly be relevant. For there seem to be few ways in which such intentions can be revealed in the photograph. For we lack all but the grossest features of style in photography; and yet it is style that opens the way to the question, Why this and not that?

Let us assume nevertheless that the photographer can exert over his image the kind of control that is exercised in painting. The question is, How far can this control be extended? Certainly, there will be an infinite number of things that are accidental. Dust on a sleeve, freckles on a face, wrinkles on a hand: such minutiae will depend initially upon the prior situation of the subject. When the cameraman sees the plate, he may still wish to assert his control, however, choosing just this colour here, just that number of wrinkles or that texture of skin. He can proceed to paint things out or in, to touch up, alter or *pasticher* as he pleases. But he has now become a painter, precisely through taking representation seriously. The photograph persists only as a kind of frame around which he paints.

The culmination of this process can be found in the techniques of photo-montage, as used by such artists as László Moholy-Nagy and Hannah Höch. Here our interest in the subject has been genuinely separated from our interest in the image, to such an extent that, as in painting, we can be entirely indifferent to the existence and nature of the originating cause. But that is precisely because the photographic figures have been so cut up and rearranged in the final product that it could not be said in any normal sense to be a photograph of its subject. Suppose that I were to take figures from a photograph of Jane, Philip and John and, having cut them out, I were to arrange them in a montage, touching them up and adjusting them until I have a telling representation of a lovers' quarrel; it represents a lovers' quarrel because it stands in an intentional, rather than a causal, relation to a quarrel. Indeed, it is to all intents and purposes a painting.

The history of the art of photography is, I believe, the history of successive attempts to break the causal chain by which the photographer is imprisoned, and to impose a human thought between subject and image. It is theory of an attempt to turn a mere simulacrum into a mode of discourse, an attempt to discover through technique (from the combination print to the soft-focus lens) what was in fact already known as art. Occasionally photographers have tried to create fictions, by arranging their models and props according to the requirements of some imaginary scenario. But a photograph of a representation is no more a representation than a picture of a man is a man.

The true talent of the camera is not to produce representations, but to provide us with surrogates and reminders. Hence, like the waxworks, it provides us with the means to realise the situations which fascinate us. It can address itself to our fantasy directly, by showing what is absent, untouchable, but real. This is surely what distinguishes the scenes of violence which are so popular in the cinema from the conventional death-throes of the stage. And it is this too which makes photography incapable of being erotic. For it represents us with the object of lust, instead of the imaginative symbol of it. The photograph is a realisation of the thing desired, and therefore gratifies the fantasy of desire long before it has succeeded in imagining and reflecting on the fact of it. The medium of photography, when bent towards the sexual and the violent, is inherently pornographic.

Of course, there are other, and better, uses for the camera. We wish for portraits of our friends, hoping to be reminded of their appearance and to renew our affections towards them. But why is the result so disappointing? In order to understand aesthetic appreciation, Wittgenstein once said, 'I would have to explain what our photographers do today – and why it is impossible to get a decent picture of your friend even if you pay £1,000'.[1] Because photography is understood through a causal relation to its subject, it is always, for us, the record of a moment: that sudden smile, that vanishing embrace, that flicker of a long since dead emotion. Painting aims to capture the sense of time, and to present its subject as extended in time. Portraiture is not an art of the momentary, and the true portraitist paints into the features of his sitter a whole narrative history. The causal relation which fixes the photographic image is a relation between events, and it is only by deserting his craft and taking up a pen, a brush or a pencil, that the photographer can adjust his image so as to break free of the moment. (This is surely what Brady manages in his famous portrait of Queen Emma.)

A photographer can aim to capture the fleeting moment which gives the most reliable indication of his subject's character. He may look in the moment for the sign of what endures. But a sign is not an expression. Someone may give a sign of guilt by blushing; but he does not thereby express his guilt. Similarly, a photograph may give signs of what is permanent, despite the fact that it cannot express it. Expression, however, is what we need in a worthwhile portrait. We can never rest content with a photo of our friend. We seek the visual narrative of his character, through which to recreate the object of our affection. Even in the realm of portraits and reminders, therefore, it is impossible that photography should displace the art of painting or even begin to compete with it.

Photography is here to stay, and will always call forth the most vigorous protests on behalf of its aesthetic pretensions.

---

1   *Lectures and Conversations on Aesthetics, etc.*, ed Barrett, p. 7.

And it is not difficult to see why. Photography is democratic: it puts into the hand of Everyman the means to be his own recorder. To defend its artistic pretensions is to make Everyman an artist. To attack them is to imply that the ability to create, to appreciate, to resonate – the ability to stand back from the world and record its meaning in an aesthetic judgement – is the property of the few. Such a thought will always be greeted as deepest heresy, in an age which builds its institutions and its monuments on the idea of human equality.

Where does all that leave the cinema? First, we must acknowledge that a film is a photograph of a drama, and that skilful use of the camera can never excuse the paltriness, sentimentality or weakness of the action. What I have said about modernism and its search for an art that will perpetuate the ethical vision, applies as much to the cinema as it does to the other arts. There are directors who have presented dramas that can be compared with the great modern works for the stage – Bergman, for instance, in *Wild Strawberries*, where an original situation, conveyed through masterly dialogue, is enhanced by dream sequences and flashbacks of a kind that can be managed successfully only through the skilful cutting that is the essential ingredient in cinematic art.

Secondly, however, we must remember the distinction between fantasy and imagination, and the inherent tendency of the camera to *realise* what it shows – to present not a world of imagination, but a substitute reality. This is never more obvious than in the case of sex and violence, and is the root cause of the fact that these now dominate the cine screen, and would dominate television too, were it not for the censor. With the aid of the camera you can realise violence or the sexual act completely, and so minister to the fantasy which has sex or violence as its focus. If fantasy breaks through the tissue of imagination, then the dramatic thought is scattered, and the imaginative emotions along with it: drama then sinks into the background, and all that we have is obscenity – human flesh without the soul.

Hence many people are quickly satiated by cinematic representations, and at the same time deeply disturbed and absorbed by features (violence in particular) which, from the dramatic point of view, have little intrinsic meaning. Imagination withers when realisation blooms, and the ethical view of our condition withers along with it. It is a significant fact that most cinema-goers are disposed to see their favourite films only a few times, and that even people whose interest is not in the drama but in the blood, screams, and orgasms have no great interest in revisiting the last occasion of excitement, and will proceed joylessly to the next one without raising the question of the value of what they watch. This contrasts with every other kind of dramatic art – theatre, novel, opera, dramatic poem – in which the perception of beauty brings with it a desire constantly to return to the source, to re-enact in our emotions a drama which never loses its point for us, since it touches the question why we are here.

The desire to make the cinema into an imaginative art form, with the camera and the cutting room as adjuncts to the drama, rather than as short-cuts to the gratification of fantasy, lies behind the great poetic experiments of the black-and-white screen. Names like Eisenstein, Cocteau, Renoir, Buñuel, Kurosawa, Mizoguchi, Bergman, Truffaut and Fellini remind us of the enormous energy that has been applied to the task of taming the camera, of teaching it to serve the drama rather than to eclipse it. It is significant that the films of those masters are almost never now seen; only a few works of blatant kitsch from Walt Disney are regularly revived, and even these are often up-dated to satisfy the increasingly jaded appetite of their viewers. The war declared by the modernists on behalf of high culture has, in the arena of the moving image, been lost. Moreover, nothing has followed the modernist experiments of Fellini, Antonioni, Polanski or Godard. What now passes for 'art' cinema is shaped by the needs of those whose taste has been formed by the screen. Hence even the most self-consciously artistic of directors will interpolate scenes of gratuitous violence or grunting sexuality into dramas which, like the screen-plays of Quentin Tarantino, will be construed in cynical and cold-hearted terms, so that the sex and the violence can be foregrounded as the true focus of the plot.

Whether the cinema can take its place alongside the other forms of high art, as a guardian of ethical ideas in an age of doubt, is not a matter that can be settled by speculation. Nevertheless, it is fairly clear that photographic images, with their capacity for the realisation of fantasies, have a distracting character which requires masterly control if it is not to get out of hand. People raised on such images – which is to say modern, or at any rate postmodern people – inevitably acquire a need for them, and seem to focus only rarely on the drama as an imaginary event, distinct from its realisation on the screen. Observing the products of the video culture you come to see why the Greeks insisted that actors wear masks, and that all violence take place behind the scenes. You also come to see that the masks are now worn not by the actors but by the viewers, and that they stay in place all day.

10
Yoofanasia

It must by now be apparent that high culture in our time cannot be understood if we ignore the popular culture which roars all around it. This popular culture is pre-eminently a culture of youth. There is an important reason for this, and my purpose in this chapter is to bring this reason to light – to show why it is that youth and the culture of youth have become so visible, in the world after faith.

Among youth, as we know it from our modern cities, a new human type is emerging. It has its own language, its own customs, its own territory and its own self-contained economy. It also has its own culture – a culture which is largely indifferent to traditional boundaries, traditional loyalties, and traditional forms of learning. Youth culture is a global force, propagated through media which acknowledge neither locality nor sovereignty in their easy-going capture of the air-waves: 'one world, one music,' in the slogan adopted by MTV, a channel which assembles the words, images and sounds which are the *lingua franca* of modern adolescents.

MTV exaggerates. There is not *one* music of youth, but many. Nevertheless, there is a particular kind of pop music, typified by such cult groups as Nirvana, R.E.M., the Prodigy and Oasis, which has a special claim on our attention, since it represents itself as the voice of youth, in opposition to the world of adults. In the music of such groups the words and sounds lyricise the transgressive conduct of which fathers and mothers used to disapprove, in the days when disapproval was permitted. But behind the anarchic words another message is encoded. This message resides not in what is said, but in what is not said, in what cannot be said, since the means of saying it have never been supplied. In the effort to give voice to this cryptic message, words float free of grammar, and become flotsam on a sea of noise. Witness Nirvana:

Was the season, when a round
Earth can do anything.
What's the reason in around,
If the crown means everything?

And then: 'How uncultured can we get?' To which question Oasis gives an answer:

Damn my education, I can't find the words to say
About the things caught in my mind.

Encrypted within the routine protest, therefore, we find another and more strangulated cry – a protest against the impossibility of protest. Trapped as he is in a culture of near total inarticulateness, the singer can find no words to express what most deeply concerns him. Something is lacking in his world – but he cannot say what. He excites his fans to every kind of artificial ecstasy, knowing that nothing will be changed for them or him, that the void will always remain unfilled. As The Verve sing: 'the drugs don't work'.

What is this thing that is missing, and for which the singer has no words? The answer is contained in the music. Melody, rhythm, harmony and tone-colour are all 'externalised': they seem to come not from within the music itself, but from elsewhere. The music is assembled with a machine-like motion, with repetition as the principal device. Rhythm is generated by percussive sounds which often have little or no relation to anything else that is happening. The music itself may draw attention to this – opening with some mesmeric sound-effect or cheesy crooning, and then bringing in the drum-kit with a barrage of amplified noise, as when a gang which has been waiting quietly on the staircase suddenly breaks down the door.

The external nature of the rhythmical force is matched by the special kind of processing given to melodic phrases. Pop melodies are made up from curt modal or diatonic phrases, with no internal variation or prolongation, and key-changes are largely unprepared. Even when pop aims to be lyrical, melody is synthesised from standardised phrases, which could be rearranged in any order without losing or gaining effect. It is not that such music is tuneless: rather that the tune comes from elsewhere, like food from the supermarket shelf, to be heated in the microwave.

What is true of rhythm and melody is true also of tone colour. The electric guitar owes much of its appeal to the fact that it is strapped on and brandished like a dildo. But it is also a machine, which distorts and amplifies the sound, lifting it out of the realm of human noises. If a machine could sing, it would sound like an electric guitar. Techno-music *is* the voice of the machine, triumphing over the human utterance and cancelling its pr-eminent claim to our attention. In such music we encounter the background noise of modern life, but suddenly projected into the foreground, so as to fill all the auditory space. However much you listen to this music, you will never hear it as you hear the human voice; not even when it sounds so loudly that you can hear nothing else. You are overhearing the machine, as it discourses in the moral void.

More significant still is the treatment of harmony. Chords are composed of notes, which stand in horizontal relations to one another, and which should therefore sing like separate voices. This has been the acknowledged basis of harmonic organisation not only in the classical tradition, but also in jazz, and in all forms of popular music before the present. But for many young people the principle has no real meaning. Part singing has disappeared from their world; the instruments immediately available to them – the guitar and the electronic synthesiser – pluck chords out of the ether with a single gesture. Whether sounded in distorted form on the electric guitar or churned out of a synthesiser, chords become relics of the harmonic thinking which first invented them. They do not move but merely replace each other, since none of their notes bears any melodic relation to its successor. A perfect illustration of this characteristic (and most of the other peculiarities of the kind of pop that I am describing) is 'In Bloom' from Nirvana's second album. The chords succeed each other in exactly the arrangement produced by moving the hand along the neck of the guitar while hitting all the strings. The resulting sequence makes sense in none of the voices, save that which generates the paltry tune.

Modern pop rarely comes to a conclusion. The music bursts out, repeats itself, and then fades away. Lacking any harmonic movement of its own, it cannot move toward anything – certainly not toward anything that requires careful preparation, like a cadence. There is, to put it another way, a lack of musical argument – a lack, indeed, of musical thought.

This externalised approach to the musical material serves a function. When the accompaniment is deprived of any melodic organisation and re-processed as noise, the singer becomes the focus of attention. The music is not designed for listening; it is designed for hearing – or rather, overhearing. It is the accompanying sound-track to a drama. The singer is projected as the incarnation of a force beyond music, which visits the world in human form, recruiting its followers in something like the way religious leaders recruit their sects. The CD often contains instructions as to where to write for further information, with a help line and support service, in the form of posters, diary items, and bulletins, like the circulars and briefings offered to its congregation by an activist church. The group offers membership. It is therefore imperative for the fan – or at least for a certain kind of fan – to choose his group, and to exalt it above any rivals. The choice is, in the end, arbitrary – or at least, not guided by any criterion of musical merit. But it is a choice that must be made. (This aspect of the sociology of popular music has been well documented by Simon Frith, who notes the ease with which the fan receives any insult to his group as an insult to himself.[1])

The fan belongs to his group, which also belongs to him. Like the totem animal of the tribe, the pop star is an icon of membership, set apart from the everyday world in a sacred space of his own. His appearance on stage is not like that of an orchestra or an actor: it is a 'real presence', an incarnation of an other-worldly being, greeted by a release of collective emotion comparable to the Dionysiac orgies described by Euripides. Tribal totems are species – and therefore immortal. By identifying with the totem you partake of its immortality, and take your place in the tribe. The pop star is an individual, but in his own way sempiternal, immortalised on disk, set against a background noise which dramatises his eternal recurrence. Hence the treatment of rhythm, melody and harmony: this processed music is

---

1   S. Frith, 'Towards an Aesthetic of Popular Music,' in Richard Leppert and Susan McClary, eds., *Music and Society: the politics of Composition, Performance and Reception,* Cambridge 1987.

like the sacred procession to the shrine, the harbinger of an incarnation.

The modern adolescent finds himself in a world that has been set in motion; he is beset by noise, by external pressures, and by forces that he cannot control. The pop star is displayed in the same condition, high up on electric wires, the currents of modern life zinging through him, but miraculously unharmed. He is the guarantee of safety, the living symbol that you can live like this forever. His death or decay are simply inconceivable, like the death of Elvis, or, if conceivable, understood as a sacrificial offering, a prelude to resurrection, like the death of Kurt Cobain.[2]

We should not be surprised, therefore, to find that, in the music of youth, singer and song are fused. Popular songs grew from a tradition of ballad and folk music, in which an expanding repertoire of favourite tunes and devices formed the foundation of music-making. Until recently the song has been detachable from the performer – a musical entity which makes sense in itself, and which can be internalised and repeated by the listeners, should they have the skill. Of course, there is a whole branch of popular music which is improvisatory. But modern pop songs are not improvised as jazz is improvised, and do not owe their appeal to the kind of spectacular musicianship that we witness in Art Tatum, Charlie Parker or Thelonious Monk. Modern pop songs are meticulously put together, often by artificial means, so as to be indelibly marked with the trade mark of the group. Everything is done to make them inseparable from the group. The lead singer projects *himself* and not the melody, emphasising his particular tone, sentiment and gesture. The melodic paucity is partly explained by this. By subtracting the melody, or reducing

---

2   See Grail Marcus, *Dead Elvis,* New York 1991. In referring the fan-star relation to totemism I am of course thinking analogically. Totemism has been a hotly disputed subject, since Sir James Frazer, in *The Golden Bough,* tried to summarise what was known about it. Freud's absurd book, *Totem and Taboo,* at least connects totemism to the conflict between generations. But it leaves the problem untouched. For an illuminating summary, see Arnold van Gennep, 'Qu'est-ce que le totemisme?' in *Religions, moeurs et légendes,* Paris 1912.

it to stock phrases that can be reapplied in any context, the singer draws attention to the song's one distinguishing feature, namely himself. The croaks and the groans with which he delivers it become the central features of the melodic line. The singer stands revealed exactly where the music should be. (Contrast here the tradition of classical performance, in which the singer is the servant of the music, hiding behind the notes that he produces.)

The harmony is surrendered to a process of distortion, involving much mixing and editing. It is therefore impossible to reproduce it by any means normally available. Sometimes serious doubts arise as to whether the performers made more than a minimal contribution to the recording, which owes its trade mark to subsequent sound engineering, designed precisely to make it unrepeatable. The music is simultaneously ephemeralised and eternally transfixed. It is an unrepeatable moment in the life of the great machine, which, by means of the machine, can be repeated forever. (When it was discovered that Milli Vanilli did not in fact perform any of the music recorded in their name, they were stripped of their Gramophone award for the Best New Act of 1990. But they lost none of their following.)

Hence pop fans find themselves deprived of one of the most important gifts of folk music – the gift of song. It is almost impossible to sing the typical pop-song unaccompanied and still make musical sense. The best you can do is to impersonate the idol during karaoke night at the local, when you have the benefit of full instrumental backing, amplification and audience, and can briefly fit yourself into the empty groove where the sacred presence lay. This intense and cathartic experience over, the fan must step down from the stage and reassume the burden of silence.

In effect, we witness a reversal of the old order of performance. Instead of the performer being the means to present the music, which exists independently in the tradition of song, the music has become the means to present the performer. The music is part of the process whereby a human individual or group is totemised. In consequence it has a tendency to lose all musical character. For music, properly constructed, has a life of its own, and is always more interesting than the person who performs it.

Much as we may love Louis Armstrong or Ella Fitzgerald, we love them for their music – not their music for them. And this is music we can perform for ourselves.

This fusion between the singer and his song promotes another and more mysterious fusion – that between the singer and the fan. You can sing the song only by becoming the singer. You are for a moment incarnate in him as he is in you. But the song is musically inept. Anybody (given the right machinery) can sing it, since nobody can. The fan knows this, and through his idolisation of the singer runs the thought: 'what has he got that I haven't?' The answer is: Nothing. To the fan in the audience the gyrating figure on the stage is himself, enjoying his fifteen minutes of fame. As he fuses with the totem the fan is transfigured, relieved at last of his isolation.

From this there follows the iconisation of the totem. Singers, groups or lead performers are not constrained by musical standards. But they are constrained by their totemic role. They must be young, sexually attractive, and with the plaintive voice of youthful desire – like the girly group called All Saints. Of course, popular musicians have always been idolised, as were Frank Sinatra, Bing Crosby, and Cliff Richard. But those old-style icons grew up in time, passed over from adolescence to adulthood, became mellow, avuncular and religious. The modern pop star does not grow up. He grows sideways, like Mick Jagger or Michael Jackson, becoming waxy and encrusted as though covered by a much-repainted mask. Such spectral creatures haunt for a while the halls of fame, trailing behind them the ghosts of their vanished fans. And then, overnight, they disappear.

Modern pop stars and groups often refuse to answer to a normal human name, since to do so would compromise their totemic status. The name must be an icon of membership. Sting, R.E.M., Nirvana, Hanson, Madonna, U2 are like the species names assumed by tribal groups, in order to clarify their social identity, with the difference that it is not biological species that are invoked by the titles, but glamorised human types.

The transformation of the pop star into an icon is assisted by the music video. This is perhaps the most important innovation in the sphere of pop since the electric guitar. The video sublimates the star, re-cycles him as image, more effectively than any

painted icon of a saint. It is expressly designed for home consumption, and brings the sacred presence into the living room.
And it completes the demotion of music, which now becomes
background, with the pop-star, transfigured into the divine status of the TV advert, occupying the foreground. The idol has entered the condition familiar from the other forms of youth art.
Like Damien Hirst and Young British Art, he has become the advert which advertises itself.

The societies studied by the great anthropologists were or-
ganic communities, bound by kinship, which sustained themselves through myths and rituals devoted to the idea of the tribe.
In such communities, the dead and the unborn were present
among the living. Rituals, ceremonies, gods and stories were the
private property of the tribe, designed to enhance and fortify the
experience of membership. Birth, marriage and death were collective and not merely individual experiences, while the crucial
process of acculturation – the transition from raw human material to a responsible adult member of the community – was
marked by rites of passage, trials and ordeals, through which the
adolescent cast off his childish wilfulness and took on the task of
social reproduction.

In the society of the anthropologists themselves (certainly of
such anthropologists as Frazer, van Gennep and Lévy-Brühl),
there existed a common store of myths, rituals and ceremonies
which created a comparable sense of the divine origin of society,
and its absolute right to sacrifice. Adolescents were instructed in
the ancestral religion, and made to respect its rites. Crucial human experiences like birth, marriage and death were still collective experiences, in which individuals passed from one state of
membership to another. Erotic feelings were regarded as the
preparations for marriage. They were duly sublimated – which
means, not idealised only, but also *ordealised*, hemmed in by
interdictions. Marriage was (as it has always been) the principal
means to pass on moral knowledge and the habits of social constraint. But all the institutions of society played their part, and
all contained their ceremonies of initiation. The transition from
adolescent to adult was marked by complex forms of induction,
which reinforced the view that all stages of existence prior to the
adult state were but preparations for it. In exploring primitive

societies, the Victorians were delighted to discover simpler and more transparent versions of an experience which lay at the heart of their own civilisation – the experience of membership, enhanced by a common religion, and by the rites of passage which lead to the full adult state, the state in which the ancestral burden is assumed.

None of that is true of modern adolescents, who have neither the tribal nor the modern urban experience of membership. They exist in a world protected from external and internal threat, and are therefore rescued from the elementary experiences – in particular the experience of war – which renew the bond of social membership. They have little or no religious belief, and what religion they have is detached from the customs and rituals that form a congregation. Television has confined each young person from childhood onwards before a box of intriguing platitudes. Without speaking, acting or making himself interesting to others, he nevertheless receives a full quota of distractions. The TV provides a common and facile subject of communication, while extinguishing the ability to communicate. The result is a new kind of isolation, which is as strongly felt in company as when alone.

Moreover the modern adolescent is heir to the sexual revolution, and to the disenchantment of the sexual act which I referred to in Chapter 2. It is impossible for modern adolescents to regard erotic feelings as the preliminary to marriage, which they see as a condition of partial servitude, to be avoided as an unacceptable cost. Sexual release is readily available, and courtship a time-wasting impediment to pleasure. Far from being a commitment, in which the voice of future generations makes itself heard, sex is now an intrinsically adolescent experience. The transition from the virgin to the married state has disappeared, and with it the 'lyrical' experience of sex, as a yearning for another and higher form of membership, to which the hard-won consent of the other is a necessary precondition. All other rites of passage have similarly withered away, since no social institution demands them – or if it does demand them, it will be avoided as 'judgemental', hierarchical or oppressive. The result is an adolescent community which suffers from an accumulating deficit in the experience of membership, while resolutely turning its back on the adult world – the world where membership is offered and received.

Now all human beings, whatever their condition, are social animals, and can live with themselves only if they also live with others. There is implanted in us the need to join things, to be a part of some larger and justifying enterprise, which will ennoble our small endeavours and protect us from the sense that we are ultimately alone. The deficit of membership must therefore be made good, but in another way – without the passage to a higher or more responsible condition. Hence new forms of 'joining in' arise. Unlike armies, schools, scout troops, churches and charities, these new forms of joining in need not involve participation – unless of a rough and undemanding kind that imposes no discipline on those who opt for them. They centre on spectacles rather than activities.

We follow the actions of our favoured team or group or idol, and adopt those actions as our own. Hence the emergence of professional sport as a central drama in popular culture. In Europe football has lost its original character as a form of recreation and become instead a spectacle, through which the fans rehearse their social identity, and achieve a kind of substitute form of membership, not as active participants in a real community, but as passive respondents in the virtual community of fans. The fan is, in some sense, a part of the group, in just the way that the football supporter is a part of his team, bound to it by a mystical bond of membership.[3]

Of course, the old tribal feelings are there just below the surface, waiting to be activated, and erupting every now and then with their usual tributes to the god of war. Football hooligans are not the peculiar and perverse criminals painted by the press. They are simply the most fully human of football fans – the ones who wish to translate the vivid experience of membership that has been offered to them, into the natural expression of a tribal right. For it must be remembered that modern adolescents are encouraged to define their own social order, their own history, their own loyalties, and their own sense of who they are. This is the logical outcome of the 'child-centred' approach to education

3   See the lyrical account by Nick Hornby, *Fever Pitch,* London 1992.

recommended by Dewey and enthusiastically adopted by a generation of teachers. The fan is trying to rescue himself from the predicament in which adults have placed him – the predicament of having to invent his own identity, in a condition where being young is the only way of being anything.

In a sense, the membership offered to the fan – in which a mesmerised passivity neutralises the desire for action – is the greatest safeguard we have, that modern societies will not fragment into tribal sub-groups, contending for scarce resources in the asphalt wilderness. For when tribal groups emerge in modern conditions, they take the form of teenage gangs, whose initiation ceremonies forbid the transition to the adult world, and are designed to arrest their members in a stage of rebellion. The first concern of such a gang is to establish a right to territory, by violently erasing all rival claims.

The teenage gang is a natural response to a world in which the rites of passage into adulthood are no longer offered or respected. Such, since the sexual revolution, is our world, and we have to make the best of it. Youth culture is an attempt to make the best of it – to make oneself at home in a world that is not, in any real sense, a home, since it has ceased to dedicate itself, as a home must dedicate itself, to the task of reproduction. Home, after all, is the place where parents are. The world displayed in the culture of youth is a world from which the parents have absconded – as these days they generally do. This culture aims to present youth as the goal and fulfilment of human life, rather than a transitional phase which must be cast off as an impediment once mature commitment calls. It promotes experiences which can be obtained without undertaking the burdens of responsibility, work, child-rearing and marriage. Hence sex, and especially sex divorced from any long-term commitment, becomes of paramount importance; so do experiences which involve no cost in terms of education, moral discipline, hardship or love – the paradigm being drug-taking, which has the added advantage that it shuts out the adult world completely, and replaces it with a cloud of wishful dreams, the very same wishful dreams that float across the screen of MTV.

I doubt that any coherent account can be given of youth culture which does not give a central place to drugs, not merely as the means to exaltation, but as the means whereby exaltation is *put on sale*. It is essential to the appeal of drugs that they are not found but purchased; and their consumption is bound up with the expertise of purchase. The person who dispenses the drug is not a priest but a salesman, and his product is etherealised and enchanted by his salesman's patter. Those who consume the drug do nothing to alter their spiritual standing; nor do they set themselves apart from other consumers. At the same time, they are offered an experience of collective elevation, a sudden release of dammed-up social feeling, as they melt into the crowd of affectionate strangers.

The resulting experience belongs to fantasy rather than imagination. It is an unreal ecstasy which also penetrates and pollutes what is real. Actual human relations, with their demands and trials and embarrassments, are blotted out by the drug, and the fantasy community meets in an unreal space where the spirit and its scruples cannot venture. It is not the soul but the body that is exalted by the drug, and sex between two bodies high on E or marijuana takes place in a world from which all demands and commitments are shut out. This is the experience that achieves a fitting encomium in Irvine Welsh's *Trainspotting*, and whose inadequacies are sentimentalised by The Verve in 'The Drugs Don't Work'.

The drug is additionally important on account of its addictive quality. Young people make a careful distinction between safe and unsafe, soft and hard, clean and dirty drugs, knowing that these distinctions are part of an elaborate ritual of pretence. For addiction both repels and attracts them. It repels because it brings ecstasy down to the day-to-day level, and removes its holiday character. But it attracts because it freezes ecstasy as permanent: the junkie is the adolescent not just stoned but set in stone. Addiction is the dead end where only youth exists, and from which you pass not to adulthood, but to death and transfiguration.

Youth culture announces itself always as radical, disconcerting, infuriating, disorienting and lawless. The group Prodigy, recently in the charts with 'Smack My Bitch Up', makes the point explicitly in its techno-slam entitled 'Their Law': i.e., the law of adults, which is there to be trampled on. But the explicit incitement contained in such a number should not blind us to the fact that transgression is also institutionalised by pop, so as to become a new conformism. The group Future Bitch, for example, announcing its debut at the Ministry of Sound – the club which is the heart of London's youth culture – declares its aim 'to disorientate its audience, pushing the current cultural scene to its limits and towards the millennium. Future Bitch,' it goes on, 'is challenging, radical, disconcerting, stimulating, unpredictable, subliminal and unprecedented'. And what could be more predictable than that?

Now there is an academic industry devoted to representing youth culture in general, and pop in particular, as genuinely subversive, a response to oppression, a voice through which freedom, life, and revolutionary fervour cry from the catacombs of bourgeois culture.[4] If the adepts of 'cultural studies' are to be believed, youth finds itself hemmed in at every point by an 'official culture' dedicated to denying the validity of its experience. On this view the profane and anarchic messages of pop are gestures of protest against a life-denying social order.

The fact is, however, that the culture of youth is the official culture of Britain, and probably of everywhere else. Any criticism of it is greeted with scorn or even outrage. Every public space in our country is filled by pop, politicians of all persuasions seek endorsement from those who produce and market it, and those who seek the few pockets of silence are an endangered species, though one that will never be protected by the conservationists. It is unsurprising that the owner and director of the Ministry of Sound, James Palumbo, is son of one of the pillars of the former modernist establishment, Lord Palumbo; unsurprising that he is a friend and advisor to Peter Mandelson (the Labour Party's leading light); unsurprising that the first role-call of guests at no. 10 after the last election included Noel Gallagher of Oasis. The culture of youth seeks and finds legitimacy with the very transgressive gestures which deny that there is any such thing. Gestures of defiance are now passports to wealth, power and fame, and a kind of ossified rudeness defines the manners of a new state-sponsored elite.

---

4   See especially George Lipsitz, *Dangerous Crossroads: Popular Music, Postmodernism and the Poetics of Place,* Verso 1994.

The youth culture prides itself on its inclusiveness. That is to say, it removes all barriers to membership – all obstacles in the form of learning, expertise, allusion, doctrine, or moral discipline. For these would be rites of passage, constituting a tacit admission that to be young is not enough, that the world expects something, and that there is a higher stage of existence to which we all must eventually proceed. This very inclusiveness, however, deprives the youth culture of human purpose. It remains locked in the present tense, looking for good causes, spiritual icons, ways of representing itself as legitimate, but without crossing the fatal barrier into responsible adulthood. How lucky it was, for those who found themselves trapped in this frame of mind, that Princess Diana should have achieved the perfect post-modern death, and been beatified by Elton John as the holy single-parent family. Like Princess Diana, the heroes of youth culture are self-advertisements, famous for being famous, but no different in the end from you and me.

It is in similar terms that we should understand the iconography of modern youth, and especially the graffiti which disfigure our cities. Most graffiti are executed in lettering taken from an expressly pre-literary source – the comic strip. Moreover, the vast majority of them do not form coherent words, nor even genuine letters. They are a kind of revenge taken against the written word, in a gesture which lays subversive claim to the very public space where the written word has for so long been sovereign, but where, thanks to TV and advertising, it is sovereign no more. The artlessness of graffiti is an act of defiance, a declaration that the knowledge enshrined in the written language is now superfluous. Remember that the written word is the most vivid symbol we possess of adult competence: it is the first obstacle set before the growing child, the original source of adult power and of the mystery of power, which in the hands of adults is propagated and exploited without force or commotion, but through signs alone. The graffiti are spells cast against the written word, designed to neutralise its power and liberate the spaces which once it occupied. Hence graffiti become badges and symbols of the new form of membership. They are the heraldic emblems of the gang. Every place disfigured by the gang's insignia is a place reclaimed from the public world. It has been privatised by youth, to become a site for the new kind of membership – membership with no rites of passage, and for the time being only.

Membership finds its ceremonial endorsement through the dance. In almost all tribal communities dancing has had an important role in reinforcing the communal spirit, and in particular in ceremonies of initiation and marriage. It represents a supreme act of surrender to the tribe and its ruling deities. In dancing we set all purpose aside and are governed by the spirit of the dance. At the same time, dancing has a peculiar social intentionality – in the normal case dancing is a 'dancing with', a fitting of one's steps and gestures to the steps and gestures of others.

In the old culture of Europe dancing was therefore a part of courtship – a kind of stylised intimacy in which the sexual allure of the body could be displayed and enjoyed without social catastrophe. For young lovers, dancing was a way of going 'part-hog', as Harold Pinter would put it, while behaving with proper decorum and with an excited consciousness of their embodiment. But it was not only young lovers who danced. Traditional dances were formation dances, like the minuet, the jig and the saraband, in which you changed partners, to find yourself dancing with someone (your grandmother perhaps) in whom you had no sexual interest whatsoever. In the Mediterranean, it was even unheard of for the sexes to dance together: the men performed in a troupe, and then the girls, each sex with an eye for the other but decorously removed from physical contact. In this way dancing became a ceremony, in which the community's bid for eternity was enacted beneath the stars.

Love, sex and the body are perceived differently by young people today; courtesy and courtship have disappeared from their dancing, since they have disappeared from their lives. The idea of dancing as an orderly affirmation of community is dead. Dancing has become a social and sexual release, among people who expressly represent themselves, in the dance, as sexual objects, even when, and especially when, they dance without a partner. Indeed the concept of the partner – of the one *with* whom you are dancing, and who agrees to dance after an exchange of courtesies – hardly engages with the new reality. You all dance together, and every step or shake or gesture is right just so long as it feels right. Nor is this new kind of dancing of marginal significance. On the contrary, it is the central episode in the youth culture, the moment when the individual renews his attachment to the group and is raised to a heightened level of excitement and a sense of the rightness of being what he is and doing what he does.

The anthropologist Arnold van Gennep coined the expression 'rites of passage' after noticing the important structural analogy between ceremonies of birth, puberty, initiation, marriage and death. The ceremonies, he argued, involve three components, ordered successively: *separation* of the individuals or groups from their previous condition; existence on the *margin (marge)* during which they remain suspended in limbo, and *incorporation (agrégation)* as participants in their new condition.[5] Thus the initiation into full membership is preceded by a period of alienation, as the youth is cast out from childhood and care, and forced to earn the fruits of adult freedom.

Imagine, however, a situation in which the adult world is clouded over: everything pertaining to adulthood has become dark, forbidding, treacherous. The only freedom lies in youth itself. Identity must be forged by the youth from his own adolescent experience – the experience of alienation, in which the protection of the adult world has been withdrawn, and nothing put in place of it. The traditional totems, which represent the continuity and longevity of the tribe, now lose their significance. The youth must construct his own totem, his own ceremonies of initiation and membership, his own sense of togetherness, while borrowing nothing at all from the expertise and knowledge of his forefathers. His dances must be formless and violent, so that only youth can dance to them; sexual pleasure, the mark of youth, must occupy the foreground of the ritual, but sex must be meticulously divorced from marriage and the birth of children. His totems must be formed in his own image – perpetually young, perpetually transgressive, perpetually incompetent.

As he dances among his kind, such a youth will be conscious of a lack. All this commotion ought to mean something; it ought to be lifting him to a higher plane. But it leaves him exactly where he was – on the margin of society, enjoying a freedom that

---

5   Arnold van Gennep, *Les Rites de passage*, Paris 1909.

is empty since it has no goal. He tries to lift himself with drugs, and as a result sinks further into the void. His protest resolves itself at last in a strangulated cry – a song which sounds like music only when the drumming feet of adolescents sound along with it. And if he discovers words for this song, they will probably be these:

I can't find words to say
About the things caught in my mind.

* * * * *

I have dwelt at length on the pop phenomenon, since it shows that there are new spiritual forces at work in the popular culture of our day. We find ourselves in a world of strange superstitions, ephemeral cults, fantasies and enthusiasms which spring from the lack of a common culture, and which may suddenly and unexpectedly crystallise, as at the death of Princess Diana. The need to belong, to be part of a group, to be inside and protected – this need is as strong as it ever was, for it is a need of the species. The vastness and mobility of modern societies have effectively destroyed the possibility of a common culture, while a process of organised forgetting is corroding high culture too. Pop culture is the spontaneous response to this situation – an attempt to provide easy-going forms of social cohesion, without the costly rites of passage that bring moral and emotional knowledge. It is a culture which has demoted the aesthetic object, and elevated the advert in its place; it has replaced imagination by fantasy and feeling by kitsch; and it has destroyed the old forms of music and dancing, so as to replace them with a repetitious noise, whose invariant harmonic and rhythmic textures sound all about us, replacing the dialect of the tribe with the grammarless murmur of the species, and drowning out the unconfident stutterings of the fathers as they trudge away towards extinction.

The gap between the culture acquired spontaneously by the young, and that which, according to Humboldt and Arnold, should be imparted in the university, is so cavernously wide that the teacher is apt to look ridiculous, as he perches on his theatrical pinnacle and beckons the youth across to it. Indeed, it is easier to make the passage the other way, to join your young audience in the enchanted field of popular entertainment, and turn your intellectual guns on the stately ruin across the chasm. Increasingly, therefore, modern intellectuals define their position as one *outside* the high culture to which they owe their status. Their task, they claim, is not to propagate Western culture, but to question its assumptions, to undermine its authority, and to liberate young people from the 'structures'. Before examining this task, we must acquaint ourselves with a peculiar product of Enlightenment high culture – the intellectual.

11
Idle Hands

The concept of the intellectual (though not the word) is new to the English language. In the past we were in the habit of distinguishing the educated from the uneducated person. And during the nineteenth century there were many educated people among our leaders – for example Disraeli and Gladstone, who between them did much to create the new style of politics, in which parties bargain for votes by promising goods that do not belong to them. But the concept of the intellectual – as a creature whose social role is shaped by his critical posture outside society – was foreign to English life. Coleridge had marked out an important role for the 'clerisy'; but he saw this class as a conservative force, maintained by church, university and the professions. The Romantic poet, the 'man of feeling', and the hermit had all been extolled and ridiculed, with Jane Austen and Thomas Love Peacock effectively putting the lid on their pretensions. Thereafter, thinking and feeling re-assumed their old functions in social life: they were useful, provided you did not notice them. The very idea that someone should draw attention to his intellect and emotions, and regard them as a qualification for overthrowing the established civil order, was anathema to the ordinary English person.

But it was at this very moment that the Russian concept of the 'intelligentsia' was first emerging: the concept of a *class* of people, distinguished by their habit of reflection, and entitled thereby to a greater say in human affairs than had been granted hitherto. The peculiarity of this class is that its members are entirely self-appointed. Nothing is demanded of the intelligentsia other than that they identify themselves as such. Having done that, they have qualified themselves for government. A few obstacles might lie in their way: but they are obstacles created by unthinking people, by the 'bourgeoisie', and can be blasted away without compunction.

That attitude led in Russia to a calamity the effects of which will be always with us. And it is worth raising the question why such a view of the intellectual life should have emerged in Russia, and why it should have had an impact there quite out of proportion to its impact in the West. Part of the answer is to be found in the nature of the Russian Orthodox Church, and the 'exit' from society which it has provided to men who are that way inclined. Those who turn their back on day-to-day life could acquire an enhanced social status as priest or monk, with an authority passed down to them from God himself. Every society needs those people – usually men – who wish to exchange the burden of reproduction for the grace of spiritual leadership; and one function of the priesthood is to impose upon them the discipline necessary to their task, and to ensure that, having made this choice, they contribute to social stability, rather than undermining it. The Russian Orthodox Church abounds in escape routes for men, and with honours and privileges which will reward their loyalty. Take away faith, however, and those privileges are no longer consoling. It is then that the dreamer becomes dangerous. Unable to enter society, and without the vision of another world that would prompt him to accept the imperfections of this one, he nurses an unstaunchable wound of resentment. His 'right divine to govern wrong' goes unrecognised, by a world that gives more credit to material than intellectual power. At the same time, he instinctively identifies with the poor, the oppressed, the misfits – those at the bottom of society, who are the living proof of its injustice. He turns against religion with the rage of a disappointed lover, and refuses to recognise the virtue of any earthly compromise. There arises the peculiar frame of mind of the exalted nihilist – a posture brilliantly described by Turgenev and Conrad, and exemplified in virtually all the characters who instigated the Bolshevik *coup d'état*.

Nihilism is not peculiar to the Russian Orthodox tradition, nor did it occur for the first time in nineteenth-century Russia. The Jacobins were pioneers of nihilism, and in the person of Saint-Just is concentrated all the senseless venom of the modern revolutionary.[1] Nevertheless, the Orthodox tradition paved the

1   See R. Scruton, 'Man's Second Disobedience', in *The Philosopher on Dover Beach,* Manchester, UK, 1990; South Bend, Ind., 1998.

way for the intelligentsia, by offering 'exit' signs on the periphery of ordinary society, and inviting the thoughtful, the sad and the disaffected to pass through them to a higher social status. Once faith had vanished, this higher status could be achieved only by threatening the foundations of society, and seizing real temporal power from those who had supposedly usurped it.

Russians always complain about the imitative nature of their culture, about their inability to come up with any ideas of their own, and their slavish adherence to Western fashions, which arrive in Moscow only when their absurdity has already been perceived in the West. In fact the current of influence has for a hundred years run in the opposite direction. The French intellectual in our time is not a direct descendent of the Revolutionaries of 1789, for all his proximity to them in outlook. He is a product of the French Communist Party, itself an import from Russia. The German intellectual lives his life in reaction to the Nazi Party, itself a perverted outgrowth of the Russian Revolution. Despite his intellectual mediocrity, Lenin has been a more decisive influence on social and political ideas in Western Europe than any other modern thinker, since it was his conception of the party which offered to intellectuals their clearest vision of their social role. The Leninist party is the new 'exit' sign. All and only intellectuals can pass through its golden gates into the social stratosphere. And in doing so they are released from earthly ties and obligations and given absolute sovereignty over the world and its goods. They rediscover their priestly role, and with it the gift of prophecy.[2] The Parisian *soixante-huitards* pretended that they had placed Gramsci on Lenin's throne. But Gramsci appealed to them only because he was a sanitised version of Lenin, offering the same vision of the Party as an exclusive club of the intellectuals, a new form of membership, above and beyond bourgeois society, and standing in judgement upon it.

The role of the intellectuals in the post-modern world is illustrated by those who emerged in glory after 1968 – that *annus mirabilis* in which the revolutionary spirit, dead in Europe for half a century, suddenly re-awakened in the midst of prosperity and leisure. These were the figures who had judged the moment

---

2   For a penetrating account of the spiritual reality of party membership, see Czeslaw Milosz: *The Captive Mind,* London 1953.

correctly, who were in tune with the *Zeitgeist*, and who had reaped their reward. Some of them were survivors from the inter-bellum – Herbert Marcuse and Wilhelm Reich, for example. Others, like Sartre, were shaped by the Second World War. Others still, like Theodor Roszak in America and Michel Foucault in France, were post-war baby-boomers, brought up during the Cold War, but without the experience of danger. All of them shared a ruling passion, which was hatred of the bourgeoisie, and of the political compromise whereby the bourgeoisie is always, so it seems, in power.

The gurus of the sixties are of great intellectual and spiritual interest.[3] But none more than Michel Foucault, who re-created the agenda of the intellectual, and up-dated the Marxist critique of the 'bourgeois' order so as to make it serviceable to the children of the bourgeoisie as they manned their toy barricades. Foucault's philosophy is conceived as an assault on 'power', and a proof that power is monopolised by the bourgeoisie. All social 'discourse', for Foucault, is the voice of power. The discourse of the opponent of power, of the one who has glimpsed the secret ways of freedom, is therefore silenced or confined: it is the unspoken and unspeakable language of those incarcerated in the prison and the clinic. Bourgeois domination is inscribed in the tissue of society, like a genetic code; and this fact justifies every variety of rebellion, while defining a singular role for the intellectual, as the anatomist of power and the priest of liberation.

If the essence of the bourgeois reality is power, and if institutions, laws, codes and cultures have all grown from a hidden agenda of domination, then it becomes impossible to accept the ruling conceptions of legitimacy. The very claim to legitimacy – whether political, moral or aesthetic – becomes the object of a corrosive suspicion. To make the claim is to stand accused of *hiding* something: it is a claim made on behalf of power, by means of a concept that power itself has forced on us. Thus arises the 'ethic of suspicion' – the duty to put in question all institutions and traditions that claim authority over the individual, and to repudiate the entire culture, in both senses of the term, which brought them into being.

3   I have examined a few of them in *Thinkers of the New Left,* London 1985.

It is impossible to confront this rooted anti-bourgeois sentiment (itself the product of the *haut bourgeois* culture of Paris) without coming clean about the fundamental, but unspoken, question: what are the possibilities for our civilisation in the modern era? What is so very wrong about the bourgeois compromise (for that it is a compromise is not in doubt), and what are we to put in its place? In short, why all this hatred?

Return for a moment to the argument of earlier chapters. The ethical life, I argued, is maintained in being by a common culture, which also upholds the togetherness of society. Local attachments feed and are fed by this culture, which is an instrument of social cohesion in both peace and war. Unlike the modern youth culture, a common culture sanctifies the adult state, to which it offers rites of passage. It therefore promises membership, as a distinct social status to which all young people can proceed; for at bottom, the ethical life is what society requires, if one generation is to care for the next.

Although a culture, understood in this sense, is vigilant towards the activities and loyalties of neighbours, it need not be xenophobic or benighted in its relations to the outer world. Indeed, our own common culture, which grew within the cosmopolitan order of the Roman Empire, under the inspired leadership of St Paul – an uprooted Jew who was also a Roman citizen – is expressly outward-going, a culture of merchants, adventurers and tradesmen, of seafarers and city-builders, for whom life among strangers is the norm. St Paul defines the Christian idea of membership by borrowing the concept of corporate personality from Roman Law: we are 'members in Christ'. The church is the Bride of Christ, and has defined itself from the outset as *katholike* – universal. In brief, Christianity offers a membership which is available to all, which promises a new life, and which is not bound by the laws of ancestors. In this, of course, it is like other cults of ancient trading and seafaring people, with many of which (notably the cult of Mithras) Christianity was in conflict during its early years.

Notwithstanding its universal claims, the Christian religion distinguishes the member from the outsider, and defines the rites of passage which safeguard social reproduction. But it differs from most religions in an important, and historically decisive, respect. The Christian religion permits and encourages legal organisation which is purely secular, and which lays claim to no divine authority. Whatever the historical cause of this – whether it be the glosses on Christ's parable of the Tribute Money, or St Paul's astute use of the Roman Law to claim protection for his new religion – the respect for secular law has made Christianity more hospitable than other faiths to the idea of secular government. The Enlightenment view of politics is already implicit in the faith which Enlightenment put in question.

Kant's description of Enlightenment, as the end of man's minority, is true; not because man grew up, but because the distinction between the adolescent and the adult state began, with Enlightenment, to fade. For two hundred years, in the midst of unprecedented social and economic change, people tried to hold on to the idea of marriage, to the rites of passage that impress upon youth the knowledge of its imperfection, and to the sexual and social discipline that would guarantee moral and political order in the face of deepening scepticism and romantic transgression. And it is those centuries of noble resistance that we mean, or ought to mean, by 'bourgeois' society. Thanks to the bourgeoisie, the show went on. Marriage, the family and high culture preserved the ethical life, in the midst of a political emancipation which – by promising the impossible – threatened the normal forms of social order.

Bourgeois society contains features which are or ought to be the envy of the world: a rule of law, which stands sovereign over the actions of the state; rights and freedoms which are defended by the state against all-comers, including itself; the right of private property, which enables me not only to close a door on enemies, but also to open a door to friends; the monogamous marriage and property-owning family, by which the material and cultural capital of one generation can be passed without trouble to the next; a system of universal education, formed by the aesthetic and scientific vision of the Enlightenment; and – last but not least – the prosperity and security provided by science and the market, the two inevitable by-products of individual freedom.

Some of these things were produced by the Enlightenment, some of them produced it. Without venturing an overview of

European history, we can agree that these social features are what we mean or ought to mean by bourgeois civilisation. They are also what the *soixante-huitards* found most hateful. For the goods that I have mentioned can be obtained only at a price – the price of loneliness, doubt and alienation. It is a price worth paying, and which would be seen to be worth paying by anyone who had studied the alternatives. Those who propose alternatives, however, never study them. They are led by hatred of the present to a blind faith in the benefits that will come from destroying it.

Bourgeois society is not the outcome of design; still less the product of a 'dominant' class or the instrument of class oppression. It arose by an 'invisible hand' from the gift of human freedom: a freedom exerted simultaneously in the economic, the social and the religious spheres. This freedom involved an emancipation from the traditional culture, and from the Christian religion which had asserted its control over personal life. But it generated the high culture which is the most reliable cure for the resulting loneliness. Bourgeois civilisation frees us from the bonds of common culture, and offers the consolation prize of art.

And that is why it is so important to Western civilisation that the old experiences of sanctity and redemption should be kept alive. For they were the price paid for our bourgeois freedoms – the way of ensuring social continuity, by withholding the most important things, the things of enduring value, from the market. The freedom extolled by Foucault is an unreal freedom, a fantasy which is at war with serious moral choice. Hence his need to desacralise bourgeois culture, and to dismiss as an illusion the real but tempered freedom which bourgeois society has achieved. Bourgeois freedom is the outcome of historical compromise. In place of this compromise Foucault invokes a 'liberation' which will be absolute, since the Other plays no part in offering and securing it.

Foucault said to one of his sycophants: 'I believe that anything can be deduced from the general phenomenon of the domination of the bourgeois class.'[4] It would be truer to say that he believed that the general thesis of the domination of the

4   *Power/Knowledge: Selected Interviews and Other Writings,*
      1972–77, ed. Colin Gordon, Brighton 1982, p. 100.

bourgeois class could be deduced from anything. For having decided, on the authority of the *Communist Manifesto*, that the bourgeois class has been dominant since the summer of 1789, Foucault deduced that all power subsequently embodied in the social order has been exercised by that class and in its interests. Hence there is nothing sacred or inviolable in the existing order, nothing that justifies our veneration or stands beyond the reach of the ubiquitous salesman.

It is worth referring to Eliot's definition of heresy, in *After Strange Gods*. For Eliot the heretic is the one who takes hold of a truth, and makes it into the supreme truth: he is the one who presses on a truth so hard that it transforms itself to falsehood. This is the process that we see in Foucault, for whom domination became so vivid a reality, as to eclipse every other aspect of the human world. It became impossible for Foucault to accept that power is sometimes decent and benign, like the power of a loving parent, conferred by the object of love. The social world, subject to Foucault's searing condemnation, was cleared of everything that redeems its ordinariness. Indeed, the heretic is the one for whom ordinariness is crime.

The 'heresy of domination', as it might be called, entered the collective conscience of the French intelligentsia, and conditioned everything that was written in the wake of 1968. Power relations, it was assumed, are also relations of oppression, and should therefore be overturned in the name of liberation. The old revolutionary call sounded again in a new voice, directed against the entire social order. The power of the law, of the father, of the teacher: all were construed as part of the 'capillary' power which flows through the channels of society. Since the very category of legitimacy belongs to 'bourgeois ideology', the distinction between legitimate and illegitimate power evaporates. In the face of power, there seems to be no honest course save transgression. The intellectuals of 1968 hunted through the social world for the marks of power, in order to declare their rebellion against it. Every gathering, every institution, every fragment of the old civilisation wore, for them, the badge of enmity. It was the sign of a power detached from that supreme diagnostic understanding of which they alone were guardians – a power which, because it was unaware of itself as such, involved the enslavement of those who submitted to its edict. The task of the intellectual was to unmask this power, to open the eyes of the victims and so, by banishing the false consciousness that leads us to accept our slavery, to open the way to liberation.

This 'unmasking' of power through critical analysis went hand in hand with a particular *conception* of power. Foucault's 'capillary' form of power moves in mysterious ways, and almost emancipates itself, in Foucault's more lyrical pages, from the pursuit of any goal. But the Nietzschean elegy to power did not appeal to Foucault's principal disciples, who saw the bourgeois *polis* as locked in the grip of a purely instrumental power: the domination of one thing *over* another, the power to achieve one's goals by the use of another's energy. Such power is linked to strength, strategy, cunning and calculation. Its principal instance is the power of the master to compel his slave – and there is working in the intellectual background that wonderful philosophical parable of Hegel's, which shows instrumental power as a necessary (though in time superseded) moment in every human relationship.[5]

The *soixante-huitards* believed that all power is of this kind. But that is not so. There are powers which cannot be used to further our goals, but which on the contrary provide our goals and limit them: such are the powers contained in a genuine culture – the redemptive powers of love and judgement. To be subject to these powers is not to be enslaved, but on the contrary to realise a part of human freedom. It is to rise above the realm of means, into the kingdom of ends – into the ideal world which is made actual by our aspiration. Perhaps the most interesting of all the tasks undertaken by the *soixante-huitards* was the attempt to show that these powers too belong to the strategy of domination. If the only end is power, then ends become means: the Kantian 'end-in-itself' is nothing but a more subtle means to domination. Hence the attack on bourgeois society cannot stop short of an attack on aesthetic value, and on the high culture

---

5   The 'master and slave' argument occurs in *The Phenomenology of Spirit*, IV.A.3. The direct influence on Foucault, however, is Sartre, specifically the Sartre of *Saint Genet, comédien et martyr*, Paris 1952.

which, by giving aesthetic form to our anxieties, also reconciles us to them.[6]

You could put the point in another way, in terms that recall Herder's original distinction between culture and civilisation. Bourgeois civilisation has gradually emptied itself of its Judaeo-Christian culture. At the heart of its institutions, therefore, is a void where the old and believing community should be. The un-believing priest cannot tolerate this void, and rebels at last against the high culture which serves to disguise it.

Thus arises what we might call 'the culture of repudiation' – the systematic examination of the high culture of bourgeois soci-ety, with a view to exposing and rejecting its assumptions. This anti-culture has grown within the very institutions that the tradi-tional high culture created, and is a last-ditch attempt to hold on to that high culture, in just the way that rebellious adolescents hold on to their parents, by acting always with a view to offend-ing them. The culture of repudiation involves a routinisation of Baudelaire's Satanism: not in order to revive the experience of sacred things, but in order to expose the experience as a sham. Hence the targets of the anti-culture are the holy things, the things marked by rites of passage, which challenge us to enter the adult world and assume its burdens.

The culture of repudiation is sometimes referred to (usually dismissively) as 'political correctness' – the assumption being that university gurus are involved in a kind of brain-washing ex-ercise, to ensure that no political views will be transmitted or ac-cepted on the campus save those of a liberal-egalitarian kind. But, interesting though this assumption is, I doubt that it has any real bearing on the cultural phenomenon. The feminists, gay ac-tivists, new historicists, crypto-Marxists, Foucauldians and deconstructionists who thrive in humanities departments do not, as a rule, have much interest in the political views of their stu-dents. Nor are they united in their opinions; nor are they very much attached to the liberal-egalitarian worldview. They are united not by their political beliefs but by a common project, and this project must be understood in spiritual terms.

6   The principal debunkers of the aesthetic, as a part of 'bourgeois ideology' are two: Pierre Bourdieu, in *Distinction,* and Terry Eagleton, in *The Ideology of the Aesthetic.* See Bibliography.

The blasphemer is not the one who disbelieves in God, but the one who is angry at himself for believing too much – the one who seeks to free himself from the divinity, and who shouts and snarls in his helplessness. The god who is a real presence at the Christian altar, is also an imaginary presence in Christian culture. Many who never take communion in fact, take communion in imagination. Such is the fate of almost every intelligent person who is brought into the ambit of Western art. Those whose task it is to teach the aesthetic legacy of Christian belief will inevitably feel drawn, not merely to its artistic achievements, but to the common culture which speaks through them, and which is no longer ours. Attachment to these things is painful, since the world no longer endorses them. And surely people are right to sense a conflict between the vision of human life that is contained in our high culture, and the liberationist philosophies of post-modern times. However widely the imagination of Shakespeare may have roamed, and however little he gave explicit endorsement to the Christian religion, his is a world in which the old common culture marks out the course of human life. It is a world of class and degree, of deference and nobility, of priesthood and kingship; a world in which women are esteemed for their fidelity and men for their prowess. It is not that Shakespeare spells out those moral ideas. They form the background to his dramas, which provide an imaginative elaboration of what they really amount to. It is inevitable that someone whose aim in life is to be 'liberated from the structures' should be in deep conflict with these sublime works of art. Their very aesthetic power lends persuasive force, and in the face of this compelling image of the lost common culture the sensitive dissident must marshal whatever weapons lie to hand, in order to cast off and neutralise its spell. The feminist, deconstructionist and Marxian 'readings' of traditional texts are therefore tributes to their power.

Moreover, since no-one really knows what liberation means, or whether life according to the new social agenda could ever be the day-to-day routine of ordinary people, the assault on the old values is the only proof we have that the new ones are viable. The high culture which enshrines the old normality is of inestimable value, since its defences are entirely contained within itself. By disenchanting its enchanted world, you score a victory which could never be achieved in the forum of everyday life, where a thousand forces conspire to sustain the *status quo*.

And here we see a connection between the culture of repudiation and the culture explored in the last three chapters – the culture of pop, corn and popcorn. Both are attempts to live without the rite of passage. The Foucauldian intellectual abhors nothing so much as the bourgeois family – the institution of social reproduction, which involves a voluntary surrender to loyalties that bind you for life, and bind you most of all when you try to discard them. Only sacred rites of passage can sustain such institutions; and the old common culture, by founding and nurturing these rites, placed social power above individual waywardness. The culture of repudiation involves a systematic, almost paranoid attempt to examine the charming images of that former life, and to cast them one by one into the pit. What is left, and what is offered to the student, is exactly what the student will have found in any case – a world devoid of sacred and sacrificial moments, in which the effort of social reproduction is no longer made.

12
The Devil's Work

Of course you don't believe a word of all that. I propose, therefore, to work through an interesting example: deconstruction,
the philosophy, if philosophy it is, associated with Jacques Derrida, the last of the *soixante-huitards* to have brought his box of
tricks to the Anglo-American university. In America deconstruction has been closely associated with the culture of repudiation,
with feminism, and with a concerted attempt to politicise the
curriculum – usually in the belief that the curriculum is *already*
politicised, though in the wrong direction. In confronting the
deconstructionist, therefore, you are not engaged in a neutral enquiry. Indeed, your opponent will say, the belief in neutral en-
quiries is not a neutral belief: it is the expression of a
conservative worldview, the very worldview that is most in need
of deconstruction.

There is no reasoned attack that does not implicitly assume
what deconstruction 'puts in question' – namely, the possibility
of a reasoned attack. In arguing with you, I assume that my
words mean something, and that their meaning is accessible to
you. I assume that I can refer to objects of common knowledge,
and that you can grasp my reference and so situate me in the
world that you too inhabit. I assume the possibility of speaking
truly, and of arguing from truth to truth, so as to carry you along
with me to a common conclusion. But if these assumptions are
untenable, then argument is futile. Moreover, by a curious inversion, my very disposition to argue jeopardises argument. That
which must be assumed in every argument cannot be justified by
argument. By pointing this out, the deconstructionist subverts
my discourse, and leaves me speechless, conscious only of his
cavernous laughter as he retires victorious into the void.

I shall therefore set deconstruction within its cultural and
political context, and try to understand its underlying agenda.
My interest is neither philosophical nor anthropological but

theological. For the ambitions of deconstruction can be fully comprehended, I believe, in no other way.

Deconstructive writing refrains from stating anything directly or assertorically. It quickly withdraws from any proposition that it sets before us, and spirals off into questions – questions which are themselves so factitious and self-referential as to deny a foothold to the sceptical outsider. Here is Derrida's response to the question whether his writings are to be judged as literature or as philosophy:

> I will say that my texts belong neither to the "philosophical" register nor to the "literary" register. Thereby they communicate, or so I hope at least, with other texts that, having operated a certain rupture, can be called "philosophical" or "literary" only according to a kind of paleonomy: the question of *paleonomy*: what is the strategic necessity (and why do we still call *strategic* an operation that in the last analysis refuses to be governed by a teleo-eschatalogical horizon? Up to what point is this refusal possible and how does it *negotiate* its effects? Why must it negotiate these effects, including the effect of this *why* itself? Why does *strategy* refer to the *play* of the stratagem rather than to the hierarchical organisation of the means and the ends? etc. These questions will not be quickly reduced.), what, then, is the "strategic" necessity that requires the occasional maintenance of an *old name* in order to launch a new concept?[1]

This is not an answer, but a series of fabricated 'meta-questions', which dance about the original question until its meaning has slipped away. If I were to describe what is really going on in such passages, I would say that their principal movement is one of 'taking back': each passage cancels in its second half what is promised in the first. Whatever enters the text enters by association rather than statement, so that no commitment is truly voiced. And once an idea has entered it drifts at once into its negation, so that the brief promise of a statement remains unfulfilled.

---

1   *Positions,* p. 71.

There are those who dismiss the result as pretentious gobble-degook, which refrains from meaning anything largely because the author has nothing to mean. And there are those who are mesmerised by it, awe-struck by its majestic vacuity, and convinced that it contains (or at least conceals) the mystery of the written word. Strangely enough readers of this second class often agree with those of the first, that the author refrains from meaning anything, and indeed that he has nothing to mean. But they regard this as a great achievement – a liberation of language from the shackles of a dictated meaning, by showing that meaning, in its traditional construction, is in a deep sense impossible.

Neither of those attitudes is exactly right. It is not right to dismiss this jargon-infested delirium as meaningless; nor is it right to welcome it as the proof that nothing can be meant. For it does mean something – namely Nothing. It is an exercise in meaning Nothing, in presenting Nothing as something that can and should be meant, and as the true meaning of every text. And that is its meaning.

Hence the deconstructive critic will not engage in philosophical argument. Deconstruction, Derrida tells us, 'determines – from a certain exterior that is unqualifiable or unnameable by philosophy – what [philosophy's] history has been able to dissimulate or forbid'.[2] In other words, it goes *behind* philosophy, which is left speechless in the face of that which it had wished to hide. The victory over philosophy comes when we show that philosophical argument is, in the end, dependent on metaphor, and that 'metaphor . . . always carries its death within itself. And this death,' Derrida adds, 'is also the death *of* philosophy'[3] – the point being that philosophy has no authority, until founded in some literal truth. Derrida is aiming for a radical 'reversal' of our 'Western tradition', and of the belief in reason that has guided it. Likewise he proposes a 'new concept of writing, that simultaneously provokes the overturning of the hierarchy speech/writing, and the entire system attached to it'[4] – the system in question

---

2   *Positions,* p. 6.

3   'White Mythology', in *Margins of Philosophy,* p. 271.

4   *Positions,* p. 42

being the intellectual tradition of which Derrida is the final and finalising product.

In other words, that there is no vantage-point from which deconstruction can be judged. If there *were* such a vantage-point, it would be philosophy; but philosophy has been deconstructed. Deconstruction is therefore self-vindicating, and provides the culture of repudiation with its spiritual credentials, the proof that it is 'not of this world' and comes in judgement upon it. Of course, the subversive intention in no way forbids deconstruction from becoming an orthodoxy, the pillar of a new establishment, and the badge of conformity that the literary apparatchik now must wear. But in this it is no different from other subversive doctrines: Marxism, for example, Leninism and Maoism. Just as pop is rapidly becoming the official culture of the post-modern State, so is the culture of repudiation becoming the official culture of the post-modern university.

Intimately connected to this posture is the belief that the human world is a human construct. To know reality is to know it through signs, and signs are our invention. If at times we have the impression that we compare our thought with the world, that we measure our utterances against the standard of some absolute reality, then this is no more than a comforting illusion, engendered by our complacent posture *within* language, and our inability to transcend language to the point where its limitations can be grasped. Thought can be compared only with thought, and the category of reality is no more than one among the many products of the intellect, a frame through which the ceaseless flow of experience is viewed. When we appear to shift from thinking to the world, in fact we shift from frame to frame.

If the human world is a construct, if the categories through which we understand reality are *all that there is*, while being also our creation, then it is open to us to un-create and re-create the world: and this will be our recreation. The existing construct enshrines and legitimates the prevailing system of power. To deconstruct it is a work of liberation, a vindication of the intellectual against his bourgeois enemy, and an 'empowering' of the oppressed. We should jettison the ruling concepts – including the concept of objectivity – and expose the oppressor whose mask they are.

I do not say that the argument has any force. Indeed it is an argument that subverts itself, like the paradox of the liar. For suppose that the argument is right. It follows that there is a distinction between right and wrong, valid and invalid, acceptable and erroneous. In which case the argument (which tells us that all such distinctions are ultimately senseless) is wrong. Nevertheless, those who pin their flag to this mast will seldom be troubled by the worm of logic, even if it has eaten the mast away. Paradox is just another subversive force; and if my own position too is destroyed by it, that leaves me all the more free to enjoy it, secure in the belief that no argument can be levelled against me, since no argument can be levelled at all.

Even if the style of Derrida and his more garrulous disciples is such as deliberately to withdraw from doctrine, making assertions, if at all, only instantly to negate them, so that the reader must either refuse to enter the labyrinth or else become entirely captive to it, there are nevertheless ideas which you are invited to register and to make your own.

The first of these is the thesis of the 'logocentric' (or 'phonocentric') nature of Western culture. Our culture, it is argued, has privileged speech over writing, regarding the spoken word as containing a truth and a reality that are irretrievably dispersed when the word is written down. Speech provides the standard to which writing must return for its credentials. This is because the self is present in the spoken word while, as every literary critic knows, it vanishes when the word is written. Hence arises a profound suspicion of the written word, which abolishes the 'self-presence' that we encounter (or imagine) in the spoken word, and substitutes an absence in its stead.

From time to time, it is true, our culture has been suspicious of the written word, and there are circumstances in which (as is only rational) it has granted privileges to speech that it does not grant to writing. But western civilisation is founded upon the written record, and its core religions – Judaism and Christianity – are, like their close cousin, Islam, religions of the book, in which Latin, Greek and Ancient Hebrew have achieved the sacred status of the voice of God, precisely through being written down: a fact that enabled them to retain their importance long after they ceased to be spoken. Our religious ceremonies involve *readings*, and our priests have also been scribes. Our worldview descends from a common culture *founded* on a sacred text. The other great cornerstone of our civilisation – the secular law – has made writing into an essential prerequisite for all important transactions, precisely because writing is a permanent sign of human intentions. And while the point of writing something down is often to guarantee the *spoken* performance, this lies in the nature of things. A parallel should be drawn with music – the greatest achievement of our high culture, and one that would have been impossible had composers not discovered that music could be *written down*, and a symphony of tones transcribed into a page of symbols.

The thesis of 'logocentrism' – that our civilisation has exalted the spoken word above all other signs – is therefore false. But this in no way deters Derrida's disciples from accepting it unquestioningly, frequently asserting it with a dogmatic conviction that closes the door to argument.[5] What appeals in the thesis is not its historical truth, but the magic light that it casts on the written text, which becomes not merely a denial of 'self-presence', but the record of an absence: an impenetrable veil drawn across the human soul, through which the reality of another life cannot be authentically encountered. The content of the text is now derived solely from our *reading* of it: the author vanishes, becomes absent; and his absence is, so to speak, read into the text, which is no more a revelation of his soul than are his discarded nail clippings. The result is an idolisation of the 'text', which can be felt in the use of that peculiar 'reifying' word to describe every work of art or philosophy, every durable 'sign'.

This idolisation is reinforced by the theory of '*différance*' – a word whose inaudible misspelling insinuates that its identity as written cannot be captured in speech. In his *Cours de linguistique générale*, Ferdinand de Saussure had argued that the meaning of a sign attaches to it only in the context of other signs that might meaningfully replace it in a sentence. It is not the sound of the word 'hot' that confers its meaning, nor any other of its intrinsic characteristics. It is the fact that it comes into play

---

5   Who are these disciples? you ask. Try Christopher Norris, *Derrida,* Fontana Modern Masters, London 1987.

through a contrast with 'cold'. The meaning of 'hot' resides at least partly in the 'difference' between 'hot' and 'cold'. (And also, presumably, the difference between hot and cold.) Saussure, Derrida assumes, is saying that language is *nothing but* a system of differences, each sign owing its meaning to the signs that it excludes. Language has no 'positive terms', but is an endless string of negations, whose meaning lies in what is not said, and what cannot be said (for to say it is merely to defer the meaning to another hidden negative). No sign means in isolation, and meaning waits upon the 'other' sign, the sign that completes it by opposing it, but which cannot be finally written down. Meaning, in other words, is never present, but always deferred, and at no point is the process of deferral *(différence)* exhausted. Meaning is chased through the text from sign to sign, always vanishing as we seem to reach it; and if we stop at a particular place, saying *now* we have it, *now* the meaning lies before us, then this is our decision, which may have a political justification, but which is in no way dictated by the text. Thus the ambiguous noun *'différence'* must be taken here in both its senses – as difference and deferral: and this too is recorded in that mysterious misspelling.

The effect of such cryptic ideas is to introduce not a critical reading of a text, but a series of spells, by which meaning is first imprisoned, and then extinguished. The goal is to deconstruct what the author has constructed, to read the 'text' against itself, by showing that the endeavour to mean one thing generates the opposite reading. The 'text' subverts itself before our eyes, meaning anything and therefore nothing. Whether the result is a 'free play of meanings', whether we can say, with some of Derrida's disciples, that every interpretation is a misinterpretation, are matters that are hotly and comically disputed in the camp of deconstruction. But for our purpose, these disputes can be set aside. What matters is the source of the 'will to believe' that leads people to adhere so frantically to these doctrines that cannot survive translation from the peculiar language which announces them.

Deconstruction is neither a method nor an argument. It should be understood on the model of magic incantation. Incantations are not arguments, and avoid completed thoughts and finished sentences. They depend on crucial terms, which derive their effect from repetition, and from their appearance in long lists of cryptic syllables. Their purpose is not to describe what is there, but to summon what is not there: to charm the god into the idol, so as to reveal himself in the here and now. Incantations can do their work only if key words and phrases acquire a mystical penumbra. The meaning of these symbols stretches deep in another dimension, and can never be coaxed into a plain statement.

Incantations resist the definition of their terms. Their purpose is not to reveal the mystery but to preserve it – to enfold it (as Derrida might say) within the sacred symbol, within the 'sign'. The sacred word is not defined, but inserted into a mystical ballet. The aim is not to acquire a meaning, but to ensure that the question of meaning is gradually forgotten and the word itself, in all its mesmerising nothingness, occupies the foreground of our attention. Here, for instance, is Derrida's explanation of the claim that reference to a present reality is always 'deferred':

> Deferred by virtue of the very principle of *différance* which holds that an element functions and signifies, takes on or conveys meaning, only by referring to another past or future element in an economy of traces. This economic aspect of *différance*, which brings into play a certain not conscious calculation in a field of forces, is inseparable from the more narrowly semiotic aspect of *différance*. It confirms that the subject, and first of all the conscious and speaking subject, depends upon the system of differences and the movement of *différance*, that the subject is not present, nor above all present to itself before *différance*, that the subject is constituted only in being divided from itself, in becoming space, in temporizing, in deferral . . .[6]

The passage adds precisely nothing to that which it purports to explain – namely, the alleged fact that reference to a present reality is always 'deferred'. On the contrary, it merely repeats the idea, in ever larger circles of self-referring and self-deferring rhetoric, with a liturgical return to the crucial words: defer, difference, *différance*. The expectation seems to be that the reader

---

6   *Positions*, p. 29.

will be induced to accept these terms as containing a meaning too vast to be transcribed in other words: a meaning that is *essentially* secret, like the meaning of a spell. Other key terms and phrases are subjected to this process: 'supplement', 'absence', 'alterity', 'mark', and the 'always already' which indicates that nature, reality and being can never be captured, since the impossibility of capturing them is 'always already' assumed in the attempt to do so.

Incantation of this kind is familiar from the religious context, and forms part of a complex social relation. In order to understand its significance, we need to supply the other four terms of the relation, namely: the idol before whom the spell is chanted; the priest who is authorised to repeat it; the deity who is summoned by it and who occupies his place within the idol; and the congregation whose membership is sealed by the sacred presence. Such we learn from the anthropologists, and their insights enable us, I believe, to understand some part of what is going on in the strange world of deconstruction. For it is evident that the 'text' is treated idolatrously by Derrida: it is lifted out of the everyday world, and endowed with a more than natural potency, a potency so great that all of reality is finally absorbed into it. It is no longer the expression of a human soul, nor in any real sense a human product, but a visitor from another realm, into which the spirit must be conjured. It is also evident that the deconstructionist critic assumes a hierophantic posture – he is the guardian and oracle of the text's sacred meaning, the unquestioned and unquestionable master of ceremonies, who displays the kind of inside knowledge, the privileged access to a secret, which the congregation must approach through him. And it is reasonable to see his readers (those to whom his words are covertly addressed) as a congregation, united by initiation and membership rather than by rational enquiry. (The 'deconstructive community' is the very opposite of the 'scientific community', in just this respect: that it is a *community*.)

We should therefore recognise the proximity of the deconstructionist milieu to the religious experience, as I invoked it in the Chapter 2. The crucial terms are liturgical, and owe their effect to repetition: to repeat them is to display a badge of membership, and to scorn or question them is to risk anathema. The normal response of those who advocate deconstruction to those who question it is not to reply with argument, but to rule both the question and the questioner out of court.[7] The critic reveals through his criticism that he is excluded from the fold. He is not *one of us*. His very disposition to argue shows his failure to understand the revelation that makes argument futile. The revelation 'transports us to a higher plane', where the infidel is deconstructed, and his assumptions deferred.

The god of deconstruction is not a 'real presence', in the Christian sense, but an absence: a negativity. The revelation of the god is a revelation, so to speak, of a transcendental emptiness, an unmeaning, where meaning should have been. Derrida is quite explicit about this (insofar as he is explicit about anything). 'Grammatology', as he originally described his gospel, announces 'the "thought-that-means-nothing", "the thought that exceeds meaning"',[8] and he elaborates the point in the following way:

> "Thought" (quotation marks: the word "thought" and what is called "thought") means nothing: it is the substantified void of a highly derivative ideality, the effect of a *différance* of forces. . . .[9]

A 'substantified void' is the Real Presence of Nothing: and this is the content of this strange religion.

Looking back over the points that I have emphasised, we can discern an underlying vision of the world that is being promoted in the form of this Real Presence, which is also an 'absence'. I do not say that Derrida himself would endorse this vision. Nor should we expect this, if my hypothesis is correct. The founder of a religion must never be entirely lucid or unambiguous; like Jesus or Muhammad, he must say a great many seemingly contradictory things. The gospel should become clear only in *retrospect*, when shaped by the requirements of a particular community, whose eager partisanship will be the proof of God's

---

7   This has been effectively shown by John Ellis, in *Against Deconstruction*, Princeton 1989.

8   *Positions* p. 12.

9   *Ibid.*, p. 49.

approval. However, it seems to me that deconstruction *has* become clear in retrospect. Those who have endorsed its claims seem also to belong to a particular congregation of latter-day malcontents: an imagined community of the dispossessed. Deconstruction has been adopted as a weapon against the 'hegemonic' and 'authoritarian' structures of the traditional culture; and it has entered the culture of repudiation as its final and clinching idea. The one thing that the deconstructionist cannot do is to endorse the powers that be, uphold Western civilisation, affirm the values of bourgeois society, or betray the ordinary conservative instincts that make the world go round – as opposed to those 'destabilising' and 'unsettling' postures which cause it to fly off at a tangent. The unspoken unity around this agenda explains the disarray that followed the revelation that one of the leading ecclesiastics (Paul de Man) had once had Nazi sympathies. It is manifestly absurd to suggest that a similar disarray would have attended the discovery that he had once been a communist – even if he had taken part in the great communist crimes. In such a case he would have enjoyed the same compassionate endorsement as was afforded to Lukács, Merleau-Ponty and Sartre. On the other hand, from the credal perspective – the perspective that examines *credentials* – the similarities between communism and Nazism are far more significant than the differences.

If the facts bear the interpretation that I find irresistible, then they offer a clear picture of the deconstructionist theology. Here it is:

(1) There is no legitimacy or authority in the world, but only human constructs, whose foundation is power.

(2) There is no truth, but only 'truth' in inverted commas: a concept that is ripe for deconstruction. All attempts to know the truth merely presuppose that we know it: and the proof that our attempt is futile is 'always already' there.

(3) There is no 'transcendental creator', nothing that produces what we perceive (the 'text') apart from those who read it. At the same time, whatever we create is also an un-creation, an absence. To know it is to deconstruct it, to show that the result of creation is also destruction. In effect, the world in which we find ourselves is an 'uncreated' world.

(4) In particular, there is no meaning. To attempt to mean something is to embark on an infinite trajectory which can never arrest itself in sense. If meaning *were* to exist, it would exist in the text – the idol. But we can summon into this idol nothing, apart from Nothing itself. The world is haunted by absence, by the Nothingness of Sartre and Heidegger: the notorious thing that noths.

(5) Thus is inverted the central idea of our religious tradition: the idea of a sacred utterance, the Word of God, enshrined in a text. The text remains sacred, but is no longer the word (the *logos*). It is the absence of the word, the 'taking back' of God's primeval utterance.

(6) However, while truth, legitimacy, authority, objectivity, meaning and reality all slip away into the void, one thing remains: the skeleton on which these masks were hung, which is power – the power of the possessor over the dispossessed, of the bourgeois over the proletarian, of man over woman, of 'straight' over 'gay'. It is at the level of power that the contest between the many readings of the text is played out. The power in question is not that of love or goodness or beauty, but instrumental power: the power to achieve one's goal, however worthless. In such power there is no virtue; on the contrary. For instrumental power contains the supreme temptation, which is to make power into its own goal, so that power is pursued for the sake of power, blind, bestial and indifferent. Such is the vision of society that Foucault sets before us, and which the *soixante-huitards* found self-evident.

(7) Against the power of the 'structures' – the power that constructed the human world and which preens itself in the masterworks of European culture – there is another that may be summoned, the power of deconstruction. The intellectual can rise above the world of ordinary meanings to the perspective that mocks them. Engage with him in contest, and he will vanish before you in a mercurial haze, only to appear at your back, laughingly pointing to your defencelessness.

In a study of Orwell's *1984 – La falsification du bien* – Alain Besançon argues that the totalitarian society envisaged by Orwell can be understood only in theological terms. For it is a society founded on a transcendental negation, a supreme 'nay-saying' to the human condition to which there is and can be no merely human rejoinder. In this society there is only power, and the goal of power is power. In the place where love should be there is absence; in the place of law another absence; in place of obligation, friendship, responsibility and right only absence. Truth is what power decides, and reality no more than a construct of power. People can be 'vaporised' – for their existence was never more than provisional, a momentary arrest in the flow of unmeaning. Language has been turned against itself, so that the attempt to mean something – the desperate bid for a significant utterance – will always fail. Newspeak deconstructs the word, so that nothing speaks (or writes) in it save power. And ruling through this power is a supreme cleverness, the Mephistophelian irony of O'Brien, who undermines in his rhetoric the very system that he serves, mockingly enforcing through torture the view that torture, like everything else, is utterly pointless.

I agree with Besançon's interpretation of Orwell, but would go one stage further. The society of *1984* is formed by projecting into reality a state of mind that exists in the actual world, and which has inhabited the brain of Western intellectuals since the Enlightenment: the religion of alienation. If people do not see what Orwell was getting at, it is not only because they have no knowledge of communist society, and no ability to imagine a system that very nearly colonised the world. Even if they do have an inkling of what went on in those places of militarised nothingness, they do not perceive the lesson contained in them. For they do not, as a rule, see that just *this* is the realisation of the intellectual temptation that sees nothing in society save power, and which deconstructs the human mask that covers it. In *1984* we see the *realisation* of what, in Foucault, is a mere idea: we encounter what it would really *mean*, for social reality to be a construct of power, and for truth to be power's minion. Orwell's Ministry of Truth offers us the key, not only to the reality of totalitarian societies, but also to the spiritual meaning of the doctrines and theories that bring them into being.

What deconstruction sets before us is a profound mystery, which can be approached only through the incantation of invented words, through a Newspeak which deconstructs its own meaning in the act of utterance. When at last the veil is lifted, we perceive a wondrous landscape: a world of negations, a world in which, wherever we look for presence we find absence, a world not of people but of vacant idols, a world which offers, in the places where we seek for order, friendship and moral value, only the skeleton of power. There is no creation in this world, though it is full of cleverness – a cleverness actively deployed in the cause of Nothing. It is a world of uncreation, without hope or faith or love, since no 'text' could possibly mean those transcendental things. It is a world in which negation has been endowed with the supreme instruments – power and intellect – so making absence into the all-embracing presence. It is, in short, the world of the Devil.

13
Conclusions

In his great valediction to Western culture – *Doktor Faustus* –
Thomas Mann portrays a composer, last true representative of
the art of our civilisation, as he wrestles with Satan. The culmination of Adrian Leverkühn's creative work will be a 'taking
back of the Ninth Symphony' – a negation of that great triumph
of Enlightenment sentiment, in which the idea of universal
brotherhood is invoked not in order to dismiss the old Christian
culture, but in order to perpetuate its ethical ideal. The Devil,
however, is a creature of the old religion. His work cannot be
understood or defined, except in terms of the common culture
which he aims to destroy. You can do the Devil's work only
where the religious motive survives. That is why the high culture
of our civilisation is his only remaining target. He works in mysterious ways – and I have tried in the last chapter to outline one
of them. But his work is also proof of the thesis that I have been
defending in this book, which is that culture is rooted in religion,
and that the true effort of a high culture is to perpetuate the common culture from which it grew – to perpetuate it not as religion,
but as art, with the ethical life transfixed within the aesthetic
gaze.

High culture and common culture can be acquired only by
initiation. Neither can be learned by sociological study or historical analysis. You are inducted into a culture, and this process of
induction is also an education of the heart. If high culture is to
survive, therefore, it must retain its critical stance: it must offer a
rite of passage to a higher world, teaching through example how
to perceive and discard our fake emotions, and how to speak and
feel with a cleaner and clearer insight into why it matters to
speak and feel sincerely. Only if you retain some of the modernist belief in the intrinsic value of high culture, will you have the
strength to impart it. Otherwise you can take one or other of the
easy options: pretend to the students that pop culture is the same

kind of thing, and join them in their blithe distractions; or show the students how to deconstruct their heritage, and reassure them that it is a burden that they have done well to discard. To do either of those things while receiving a state-funded salary is a great achievement, and one proof that our universities are not entirely devoid of intelligent people.

But how should culture be taught? Arnold enjoined us to recommend 'the best that has been thought and said', and to encourage a critical response to it. But who is to say what is best? The curriculum assumed by Arnold is now denounced as 'monocultural', 'patriarchal', an instrument of ideology and class oppression. In place of it we are urged to adopt a multicultural curriculum, which will remove the social and political prejudices that spoil the great works of the past.

That outlook is founded, however, in a confused conception of culture. If you mean by culture what I have called common culture, then such a thing cannot be imparted as a free choice among alternatives; it cannot be divorced from the social and political postures which define the life of the community. There is no such thing as a multicultural education when the goal is religious belief. If however you mean by culture what I have called high culture, then the complaints are without force. Our high culture is a culture of Enlightenment. It invokes an historical community of sentiment, while celebrating universal human values. It is based in the aesthetic imagination, and spontaneously opens itself to human possibilities other than those contained in its religious root. It draws from this root a wealth of human feeling that it spreads impartially over imagined worlds. From *Orlando Furioso* to Byron's *Don Juan,* from Monteverdi's *Poppeia* to Longfellow's *Hiawatha,* from *The Winter's Tale* to *Madama Butterfly,* our culture has continuously ventured into spiritual territory that has no place on the Christian map.

The humanities, as these emerged in the nineteenth-century university, were not designed to instil a common culture. On the contrary, they assumed the work of 'acculturation' to be already complete. Their purpose was to *reflect* on the human world, by providing images, stories, works of art, and expressions that would become part of the mental repertoire of those who absorbed them. The resulting curriculum was far from monocultural. Our ancestors studied – and I mean *really* studied – cultures that were entirely strange to them. They learned the languages and literature of Greece and Rome, came to understand, love and even in their own way to worship the pagan gods; translated from Hebrew, Sanskrit and Arabic, and roamed the world with an insatiable curiosity, believing on the best of grounds that nothing human would be alien to them. It was second nature to the nineteenth-century graduate to learn the language of a country to which he travelled, to study its literature, religion and customs – often to the extent of going native, like many of the British in India and many of the Indians in Britain.

The advocates of a multicultural curriculum ought to propose Anglo-Indian literature, from Kipling and Tagore to Paul Scott and Vikram Seth, as compulsory reading. But if you look at their schemes, you will find no mention of this literature, or of anything like it. A work like *Kim* is a work of high art, which speaks to the cultivated mind, and can be understood only by the reader who responds critically to aesthetic values. Instead of such works, a mish-mash of pop, soap-opera and pre-emptive kitsch is proposed as the curriculum that will do justice to the many cultures that live and thrive in a modern city. But of course, it does justice to none of them, for it imparts only the culture that young people would absorb in any case – a culture without judgement, which is therefore incapable of imparting the knowledge on which the ethical life depends. Only if we teach the young to criticise do we really offer them culture. Otherwise what we call culture is a collective mental indolence.

And that is why the old curriculum has been discarded: not because it was burdensome, but because it was shaped by criticism. If interpretation is misinterpretation and there are no values, criticism makes no sense. The search for aesthetic value, and the ethical life that it celebrates, is a futile search. If that is so, how should culture be taught? The answer is evident: not by inducing it, but by observing it from a point of view outside. Criticism gives way to 'theory', and theory includes every device that might be used to undermine the authority of 'Western culture'.

Hence, although nobody knows what the next burst of 'theory' will amount to, we know that it will be part of the culture of repudiation. Theory repeats, in opaque and solidified prose, the assault on bourgeois values, patriarchy and the 'official' culture that was led by the *soixante-huitards*. To encounter theory is to enter the literary equivalent of a socialist-realist museum, where concrete workers stand side by side with concrete intellectuals, punching their way into the future with clenched concrete fists. Deep within the lightless prose the old political message heaves and groans: culture is ideology, and ideology is the mask of power. Reduced now to a helpless tautology, this last vestige of belief, uttered in the world beyond belief, provides the core idea of 'cultural studies'.

Rather than take the reader on a tour of this lugubrious museum I shall bring one of the exhibits into the light and dust it off for a critical inspection. Here is (the reader must take my word for it) an exemplary sentence of theory, which will illustrate the advances made by 'cultural studies' in the postmodern era:

> If twentieth-century theory has valuably enforced the awareness of the excessiveness of value, the endless surpassing, in fact and possibility, of the values and thematics of value dominant in Western culture, then it is also necessary to constitute a political discourse which could secure and nurture the permanent possibility of this reflexive surpassing of value.

What is most curious about this sentence is not the muscle-bound political posturing, but the syntax in which it is enclosed. This syntax derives from an over-arching 'if-then' in which there is no relation whatsoever between antecedent and consequent, and no sense that the first is really hypothesised, rather than dogmatically asserted. The sentence illustrates a peculiar use of the word 'if', not to put something in question, but to protect it from questioning. The sentence also lays claim to a sovereign authority over its subject – a comprehensive vision of the 'twentieth-century' and the 'Western culture' that shows their historical meaning. It reinforces itself with abstract notions, which it also 'reifies' into things and processes. The sentence is infected by a whirring factory-like dynamism: the abstract notions are doing things and changing things. Thus 'twentieth-century theory' becomes a kind of policeman, who 'enforces' an 'awareness' (though 'valuably'); while 'political discourse' can 'secure and nurture' some other, equally abstract, result. At the same time we find a veering away from meaning. 'Values' are 'surpassed', and surpassed, moreover, in 'fact and possibility'. Anyone who puzzles over that phrase will not be reassured to find that 'values' are at once edged out by 'thematics of value'. The 'surpassing of values' which is first offered as a fact, and then as a possibility, finally becomes something to be 'secured and nurtured', as a possibility which is 'permanent'. But it has now become a 'reflexive' surpassing – thereby implying that values are in the business of surpassing themselves. In which case, who is being exhorted to do what, in response to the phrase 'necessary to try'?

Note too that the operative words are carefully concealed like the gun in the holster, and brought out only as the sentence rounds the corner towards its syntactical apotheosis. Whatever this gobbledegook means, the author implies, it is pointing towards 'political discourse' – and the Foucauldian jargon is sufficient to elicit the nod of easy assent from his intended readership.

Lest you should think that I have unfairly taken a sentence out of context, here is another, chosen more or less at random from the same work. You will see that the syntactical devices that I have remarked upon are inseparable from the writer's thought:

> If cultural modernism takes the form of an extreme differentiation of the value of culture and the arts, along with the gradually consolidated (and increasingly implausible) claim that artistic value is identical with value *as such*, then the academic study of cultural and artistic practices has provided an institutional embodiment of this differentiation.

Rather than puzzle over the meaning of such a sentence, one should respond instead to its style. The sentence reads as an 'inspoken attack' – a vehement whisper of disaffection, which is addressed, however, only to those who already share the writer's viewpoint. The context tells us that the object of disaffection is the usual one – Western culture, and the habit of evaluation which created it. But this object is hidden: to expose it too evidently to view would be to invite refutation. And in the postmodern academy neither affirmation nor refutation have a place. Rational discussion, after all, is the prerogative of the *old* curriculum, the ideological mask of patriarchal power.

There are many reasons why people seeking tenure in an academic institution should cloak their writings in a mantle of pseudo-science. But there is more to 'theory' than half-naked ambition. Theory is the theology of repudiation. Like other theological enterprises, it conceals its most vulnerable assumptions behind mind-numbing disputes, whose meaninglessness can be discovered only by the kind of diligent study which outsiders have no time for. In the new academy, as in the medieval university, there are tenets which are not to be questioned since they define the community – the community of the unfaithful. Feminism, gay liberation, the belief in the equality of cultures, and the relativity of values: these community-forming assumptions are carefully protected from criticism by embedding them in the very syntax of debate.

This is not the place to question those assumptions. But it is worth pointing out that it is futile to defend Western culture by attacking feminism, gay liberation and the other movements which have captured the curriculum. For these movements are the effect and not the cause of cultural uncertainty. And this uncertainty occurs not at the level of the curriculum, but at the level of social reproduction. The loss of the transition from youth to adulthood means the loss of sexual restraint, and therefore the loss of trust between the sexes. The sexes cease to be partners and become rivals. By repudiating the old culture the feminist forestalls the grief of losing it. And from the personal point of view, this strategy is the right one.

Why are rites of passage important? Why should we strive so hard to forbid the easy avenues and the fake emotions? Why should we teach the young to match their emotions to the examples given by art and religion, and to compare worldly experience with its idealised completion? Why not let humanity float along the air-waves in peace, and take our place in the community of unbelievers, burying our hopes, like theirs, in some monument of solidified 'theory'?

Perhaps an answer is suggested by this book. We have abundant scientific knowledge of our world and technical mastery over it. But its meaning is hidden from us. We have knowledge of the facts, and knowledge of the means, but no knowledge of the end. My purpose in this book has been to illustrate this peculiar ignorance – not ignorance *that*, or ignorance *how* but ignorance *what*. We no longer know what to do or what to feel; the meaninglessness of our world is a projection of our numbness towards it. Culture supplies what is missing – the knowledge what to feel which comes with the invocation of our true community. The community may vanish in fact, but live on in imagination. And that is the point of high culture: neither to 'do dirt on life', nor to emphasise its senselessness, but to recuperate by imaginative means the old experience of home.

Social reproduction is not guaranteed by the species. Of course, men and women will always produce children. But they may not always make a home for them. Many young people enter the world without any real commitment from their parents. They have no religious beliefs but only blind superstitions; no adult role models but only the experience of strangers, who play at mum or dad for a while and then leave as they came, without an explanation. Their social aspirations are derived from adverts and pop, and no gratification is forbidden or postponed for long enough to offer a vision of the higher life – the life of sacrifice, in which the sacred has a place. Only a rite of passage, offering the transition to difficult and previously forbidden things, can lift human beings from this predicament. Without it, they remain savage, incapable of receiving or passing on the inherited capital of moral knowledge. It is precisely the experience of passage, from emotional isolation to full and answerable membership, that a high culture strives to perpetuate.

Published just after the First World War, Oswald Spengler's *Decline of the West* presents a 'comparative morphology' of cultures. 'The West', Spengler argued, has come to its end, as every culture must. We have now entered the period of mere 'civilisation', when administration and technology take over from the flowering of the spirit in its summer forms. That is Spengler's account of the Enlightenment, phrased once again in terms of Herder's distinction between *Kultur* and *Zivilisation*. Our culture rose to its self-conscious height in the time of Goethe, who captured its spirit in *Faust*. Thereafter, Spengler believed, it rapidly died, to be replaced by the cold routines of a civilisation destined, at last, to crumble to nothingness, as its structure rots away.

I have had nothing positive to say about popular culture, and nothing positive to say about the cultural establishment. My conclusions, however, are not so grim as Spengler's. We have entered, as I see it, a spiritual limbo. Our educational institutions are no longer the bearers of high culture and public life has been deliberately moronised. But here and there, sheltered from the noise and glare of the media, the old spiritual forces are at work. Popular culture contains pockets of gentleness and melody. Architects, writers and composers produce works which are neither kitsch nor 'kitsch'. Prayer and penitence have been interrupted, but not forgotten. To those who wish for it, the ethical life may still be retrieved. Ours is a catacomb culture, a flame kept alive by undaunted monks. And what the monks of Europe achieved in a former dark age, they might achieve again.

Let us return for a moment to Wagner. By living the life of heroic passion, the composer tells us, we incarnate the divine. It is not we who seek redemption through the gods, but the gods who seek redemption in us, achieving the only reality of which they are capable – their momentary presence in the human sacrifice which summons and destroys them. The gods are bound in the knot which the myth has woven. We are free – free, however, only to renounce our freedom in the vow of love, and then to renounce life itself, when love demands it.

The artistic goal is to make us recognise that we can live *as if* that higher life – the ethical life *in extremis* – were ours. But, as I argued earlier, there is a flaw in the Wagnerian ethic. The intensification of passion at which Wagner aims situates love outside the cycle of reproduction; love announces the death of the lover and the extinction of the moral force that lives in him. We need the Wagnerian 'as if'; we need the vision of ourselves as ennobled by our aims and passions, existing in ethical relation with our kind. But we must free ourselves of those last romantic illusions – including the illusion that love is the answer. Love is not the answer, but the question, the thing which sets us searching for meaning in a world from which meaning has retreated. How then, should we live, when we live beyond belief? 'What remains when disbelief is gone?'

Light comes from the East. The Chinese sage Confucius, who lived five centuries before Christ, left no writings of his own, and is known to us, as Christ is, from the words and deeds recorded by his apostles. Unlike Christ, however, Confucius was not a religious reformer, but an ardent conformist in all matters both temporal and spiritual, and his counsels and maxims, recorded in the *Analects*, are concerned with the orderly conduct of life in *this* world, rather than with hopes and fears for the next. Confucius lived through the collapse of feudal civilisation in ancient China, and wandered the land in search of a prince who would listen to his counsels. He loved life, was fond of horses and hunting, and was both a practical and a respectable man, distinguished from his contemporaries largely by his propensity both to utter uncomfortable truths, and to live by them.

Confucius deplored innovation, scorned the idea of human progress, and hoped for a race of human beings who would place learning, study and ceremony before pleasure, profit and power. His was a profoundly backward-looking philosophy, which honoured the past above the present, and traditional authority above usurping power. Immemorial custom meant more to him than exciting new ideas: indeed, the newer and more exciting an idea the more suspicious he was of it; and his emphasis on filial piety and punctilious obedience was tempered by no phoney compassion for those who could not or would not conform.

In the delightful and unfussy footnotes to his translation of the *Analects*, Simon Leys compares Confucius's situation to ours. We too are living 'at the end of things', witnessing the collapse of moral order, and a loss of piety among the young. We too need the Confucian virtues of humanity, obedience, and respect for custom and ceremony. The Master feared that people would acquire a taste for the 'music of Zheng', that they might become 'dishevelled savages who fold their clothes on the wrong side', that they might spend less than three years in ritual mourning for their parents. How lucky we should be, if we feared nothing worse than that. Nevertheless, Confucius was right to connect the disrespect for parents with the downfall of empires. His summary of the matter is inimitable:

> The Master said: "I detest purple replacing vermilion; I detest popular music corrupting classical music; I detest glib tongues overturning kingdoms and clans".

For 'vermilion' read the old uniforms of office, for 'purple' read baseball caps, for 'glib tongues' read the media. But what was the Master's answer? He did not, like Kierkegaard, summon us to the leap of faith:

> Someone asked for an explanation of the Ancestral Sacrifice. The Master said: "I do not know. Anyone who knew the explanation could deal with all things under Heaven as easily as I lay this here"; and he laid his fingers upon the palm of his hand.

Confucius did not offer any metaphysical system or religious creed. Instead he enjoined us to live *as if* it matters eternally what we do: to obey the rites, the ceremonies and the customs that lend dignity to our actions and which lift them above the natural sphere; to cultivate the heart and the tongue so that beauty is always in and around us; and to live in the condition which Wordsworth called 'natural piety', acknowledging the greatness of creation, and the imponderable mystery of time. In this way, even if we have no religious beliefs, we acknowledge the existence of sacred things, and endow our gestures with a nimbus of the supernatural. Living thus we peer serenely into the eternal. And if you ask what it is *like* to live thus, then listen to the closing bars of Mahler's *Das Lied von der Erde* – a setting of an old Chinese poem, imbued with the spirit of Confucius, and incidentally a beautiful proof that Western culture, unlike Chinese culture, is radically multicultural.

Confucius was unable to find his Philosopher King, and died without hope for the future of civilisation. Subsequent history, however, confounded his predictions, and showed that a philosopher ought to say what he thinks, especially at a time when no-one who is anyone agrees with him. For Confucianism became the official outlook of the greatest Empire that the world has known. Confucius did not give us faith; but he gives us hope.

Quite Interesting Bibliography

The following bibliography includes works that were referred to in my argument, either expressly or implicitly, together with other works which contribute to the understanding of modern culture.

Anderson, Benedict, *Imagined Communities,* London 1983, revised edn. 1991, an examination of the process whereby tribes turn themselves into nations in the post-colonial world.

Aristotle, *Nicomachean Ethics,* for the connection between moral virtue and the education of the emotions.

Aristotle, *Poetics,* for the theory of tragedy as 'catharsis'.

Arnold, Matthew, *Culture and Anarchy,* being the classic presentation in English of the case for high culture in a world without faith.

Austen, Jane, *Sense and Sensibility* and *Northanger Abbey,* for the sly demolition of romanticism as a purveyor and traducer of religious thrills.

Barthes, Roland, *Le degré zéro de l'écriture,* Paris 1964, (tr. *Writing Degree Zero,*) pretentious statement of 'structuralist' principles in criticism.

Baudelaire, Charles, *Les fleurs du mal,* his artistic triumph, and the first clear voice of the modernist poet.

Baudelaire, Charles, *Le peintre de la vie moderne,* Baudelaire's defence of Manet and the unofficial art of his contemporaries; contained in most collections of Baudelaire's critical writings.

Baudrillard, Jean, *La société de consommation,* Paris 1970, Foucauldian attack on consumerism by a master ironist who in more recent work has succumbed to it.

Baumgarten, A.G., *Aesthetica,* 2 vols. (Frankfurt-an-der-Oder, 1750–58); the first modern use of the term 'aesthetic': a curious work, not without interest, concerned largely with the problem of poetic meaning.

Benedict, Ruth, *Patterns of Culture,* London 1935, leading work of a Spengler-influenced anthropologist who views common culture as the form or pattern through which a community achieves coherence; contains important discussions of the interaction between religion, ceremony and membership.

Besançon, Alain, *La Falsification du bien,* Paris 1988, tr. Matthew Screech, *The Falsification of the Good,* London 1996, a study of Soloviev and Orwell, and of the spiritual meaning of the totalitarian thought-process.

Bloom, Harold, *The Western Canon,* New York 1994, a prodigiously learned attempt to summarise the high culture of Western civilisation, and to say why it matters.

Bourdieu, Pierre, *Distinction: A Social Critique of the Judgement of Taste,* tr. Richard Nice, London 1984, which contains an attempt (in an appendix) by an old *soixante-huitard* to relegate Kant's *Critique of Judgement* to the category of 'bourgeois ideology'.

Brann, Eva, 'Jane Austen', a lecture delivered at the State University of Minnesota, Annapolis in 1975. I don't know where I dug this up or how I would rediscover it; but a moving work by a civilised critic.

Broch, Hermann, *Dichtung und Erkennen,* Frankfurt, 1976, collected criticism by a meditative novelist who never could see the bright side of anything.

Burke, Edmund, *Reflections on the French Revolution,* prescient analysis of the French Revolution, a moving critique of the Social Contract theory, and an oblique affirmation of common culture as the heart of social and political order.

Chailly, Jacques, *The Magic Flute, Masonic Opera,* London 1972, an interesting attempt to unpack the symbolism of Mozart's masterpiece.

Coleridge, Samuel Taylor, *Biographia Literaria,* Everyman Edition, ed. George Watson, London 1956, literary criticism which is also a philosophy of life, and which grows out of and in opposition to the Romanticism of its author.

Collingwood, R.G., *Principles of Art,* Oxford 1938, an attempt to see the enterprise of modernism in terms of Croce's aesthetics.

Connor, Steven, *Theory and Cultural Value,* London 1990, a pertinent instance of 'theory', written by a literary scholar in the midst of it, and the mist of it.

Conrad, Joseph, *Under Western Eyes,* and *The Secret Agent,* two novels which capture the negativity of revolutionary sentiment.

Croce, Benedetto, *Aesthetic, as Science of Expression and General Linguistic,* tr. Douglas Ainslee, New York 1922, for the classic attempt to distinguish expression from representation, and to identify the first as the aim of art, the second as its potential enemy.

Derrida, Jacques, *Positions,* tr. and ed. Alan Bass, London 1987; *Margins of Philosophy,* tr. Alan Bass, Brighton 1982, and . . . no, that will do.

Dilthey, Wilhelm, *Selected Writings,* tr. and ed. H.P. Rickman, Cambridge 1976, from which you will discover that Dilthey is very much weaker than his one big idea.

Durkheim, Emile, *Les formes élémentaires de la vie religieuse,* Paris 1912 *(Elementary Forms of the Religious Life),* the best effort that I know to give an anthropology of religion, and to show why religion is inescapable. I have drawn on this great work in Chapter 2.

Duteurtre, Benoît, *Requiem pour une avant-garde,* Paris 1995, devastating survey by a musician-novelist of the modernist musical establishment in France, and its stifling effect on the national culture.

Eagleton, Terry, *The Ideology of the Aesthetic,* Oxford 1990, neo-Marxist debunking of the aesthetic. The last gasp of the sixties.

Eliot, T.S., *The Waste Land,* his modernist poem, the footnotes of which are a useful guide to the anthropological literature which casts light on our predicament.

Eliot, T.S., *Four Quartets,* Eliot's homecoming from his prodigal wanderings, in which he plays the parts of father, son and fatted calf.

Eliot, T.S., *Selected Essays,* London 1932, the works of criticism which did most to re-shape the canon of English literature in accordance with the modernist's strict dietary requirements.

Eliot, T.S., *After Strange Gods,* London 1934, three lectures published in the thirties and since then allowed to go out of print, possibly because of subsequent allegations of anti-Semitism.

Eliot, T.S., *On the Use of Poetry and the Use of Criticism,* London 1933, 2nd edition 1964, in which Eliot confronts the problem of poetry and belief, discussed in Chapter 4 of this book.

Eliot, T.S., *Notes Towards the Definition of Culture,* London 1950, a strange book, in which Eliot nevertheless identifies, perhaps for the first time, the religious nature of culture in all its forms.

Ellis, John, *Against Deconstruction,* Princeton 1989, a workmanlike demolition of deconstruction in its academic heyday, as liable to make converts in the academic world as Billie Graham in rural Afghanistan.

Feuerbach, Ludwig, *The Essence of Christianity,* tr. George Eliot, New York 1957, the book which tried to spell out what follows, if the gods are our creations.

Fichte, J.G., *Addresses to the German Nation,* 1807–8. It needed saying at the time.

Foucault, Michel, *Birth of the Clinic, Les Mots et les choses, Surveiller et punir, History of Sexuality, Power/Knowledge,* works devoted to rewriting modern history, including the history of ideas, institutions and sexual mores, as the history of 'bourgeois' power.

Freud, Sigmund, 'Mourning and Melancholia', in *Collected Papers,* tr. Joan Rivière, London 1925, vol. 4, in which the founder of psychoanalysis says wise things about the process – the 'work of mourning' – through which we all must go, if we are to accept the death of things we love.

Freud, Sigmund, *Totem and Taboo,* 1913, in which Freud says far less wise things about the structure of primitive societies, and sees the totem as a symbol of the primeval father, murdered so that his sons could enjoy his wives, and re-murdered ceremonially as an expiation of guilt.

Frith, Simon, *Performing Rites,* Oxford 1996, one of several studies of pop in which Simon Frith bravely tries to discern something in it.

Gramsci, Antonio, *Selections from the Prison Notebooks,* ed. Hoare and Smith, New York 1971, sacred text of 1968, written by one of the few Communist Party leaders who never had a chance to kill anyone. Gramsci's theory of culture as part of the 'hegemony' of a ruling class is of abiding relevance.

Greenberg, Clement, 'Avant-garde and Kitsch', in *Partisan Review,* 1939. The essay which set the agenda for the modernist establishment.

Hegel, G.W.F., *The Phenomenology of Spirit,* tr. A. Miller and J.N. Findlay, Oxford 1977, containing his account of culture as *Bildung,* one 'moment' in which is the contest between master and slave.

Herder, J.G., *Outlines of a Philosophy of the History of Man,* tr. T.O. Churchill, 2nd Edn., 2 vols., London 1803, containing Herder's diffuse account of culture, as the binding force of a people and its history.

Hirsch, E.D., Jr., *Cultural Literacy,* New York 1988, in which a staunch defender of the old curriculum tries, but without much success, to say why it matters.

Hornby, Nick, *Fever Pitch,* London 1992, romantic and charming invocation of the world of a football fan, with astute anthropological observations along the way.

Humboldt, Wilhelm von, ed. Marianne Cowan: *Humanist without Portfolio: an anthology,* Detroit, Mich., 1963, a selection from this advocate of a liberal-humanist culture.

Jung, Carl G., *The Archetypes and the Collective Unconscious,* tr. R.F.C. Hull, London 1959, for a wishful account of myth which brings the aesthetic and the religious together.

Kant, Immanuel, *The Critique of Judgement,* the third of Kant's great critiques, available in several hopeless translations, and not much clearer in the original, which nevertheless puts aesthetic judgement for the first time at the centre of our modern intellectual concerns.

Kant, Immanuel, 'An Answer to the Question: "What is Enlightenment?"', in *Political Writings,* tr. H.B. Nisbet, ed., Hans Reiss, 2nd edn., Cambridge, 1991, in which the philosopher gives his celebrated but empty definition of the movement which would have been the salvation of mankind if only Kant had been in charge of it.

Kant, Immanuel, *Perpetual Peace,* available in various translations. The idyll of international peace founded on moral law and republican constitution. The political credo of the Enlightenment.

Kierkegaard, Søren, *Either/Or*, tr. Swenson and Swenson, New York 1959, an inspired vision of what happens to the ethical life, when it falls under the aesthetic gaze.

Kierkegaard, *Concluding Unscientific Postscript*, tr. Swenson and Lowrie, London 1941, in which the 'leap of faith' becomes a leap into subjectivity and self-hood.

Leavis, F.R., *The Great Tradition, New Bearings in English Poetry, The Common Pursuit, Nor Shall my Sword*, and a few more, which between them constitute the greatest attempt in our century to rescue culture from the world of mass sentiment, and to acknowledge its moral and spiritual importance. I also refer to the contributions that Leavis made to the journal that he edited, *Scrutiny*, two volumes of selections from which, edited by Leavis, were published by Cambridge University Press in 1966.

Lévi-Strauss, Claude, *Totemism*, tr. Rodney Needham, London 1964, an attempt to dismiss the problem of totemism, by showing that there is no such thing – or at any rate no single thing. Totally unpersuasive, but a useful survey of the controversy.

Leys, Simon, tr. and ed., *The Analects of Confucius*, London 1996, which tells us how to rediscover piety without religious belief.

Lipsitz, George, *Dangerous Crossroads: Popular Music, Postmodernism and the Poetics of Place*, London 1994, preposterous post-modern pastiche of professorial pedantry.

Lodge, David, *Small World*, London 1984, a fictional account of the world of academic English in the late twentieth century; a useful guide to the politics of literary theory.

Maine, Sir Henry, *Ancient Law*, Oxford 1861, which contains much more than the distinction between status and contract.

Mann, Thomas, *Doktor Faustus*, the last gasp of the German idea, unless you count *Felix Krull* (unfinished) and Strauss's *Four Last Songs*.

Marcus, Grail, *Dead Elvis*, New York 1991, on a particular instance of modern totemism.

Marx, Karl and Friedrich Engels, *The German ideology,* exuberant first shot at the theory of ideology, in which culture is caricatured as a functional by-product of capitalist 'relations of production', part of the ideological disguise of bourgeois power.

Marx, Karl, the 1844 manuscripts, extracted in most editions of Marx's Selected Works: the classical source for the 'alienation' idea, and the borrowings from Hegel, Schiller and Feuerbach. The greatest single influence on the culture of modern universities, and none the better for that.

Marx, Karl, *Capital,* vol. 1, for the theory of commodity fetishism.

Milosz, Czeslaw, *The Captive Mind,* tr. Jane Zielonko, London 1953, the best antidote to Marx and Marxism and a disturbing account of mental and moral corruption.

Nietzsche, F.W., *The Genealogy of Morals, The Twilight of the Idols, The Case of Wagner, The Birth of Tragedy,* and *Wagner in Bayreuth* – all seminal texts about modern culture, from a writer who both hated it and loved it.

Norris, Christopher, *Derrida,* Fontana Modern Masters, London 1987, an amusing illustration of Derrida's spell-binding quality.

Peacock, Thomas Love, *Headlong Hall,* for a debunking of romantic sensibility and the culture of feeling.

Pound, Ezra, *The ABC of Reading,* if only to see why reading matters.

Praz, Mario, *The Romantic Agony,* tr. Angus Davidson, London 1933; the original Italian title tells us more about the real contents of this book: *La carne, la morte e il diavolo nella literatura romantica,* Milan 1930. A dated but distinguished account of the romantic conjunction of love, death and transgression.

Rosenberg, Harold, *The Tradition of the New,* New York, 1972. One honest critic's attempt to stay on the side of modern art through thin and thinner.

Saussure, Ferdinand de, *Cours de linguistique générale,* Paris 1966, a dated and obscurantist work which nevertheless achieved an influence out of all proportion to its merits, on account of the obscurantists who borrowed from it.

Schiller, Friedrich, *Letters on the Aesthetic Education of Man,* tr. E. Wilkerson and L.A. Willoughby, Oxford 1967, which was perhaps the first attempt to describe high culture as an aesthetic phenomenon, and to deduce its social and political importance from that.

Schiller, Friedrich, *Über naïve und sentimentalische Dichtung* (Naive and Sentimental Poetry), Grossherzog Wilhelm Ernst Ausgabe, Leipzig 1906, vol. 4, pp 532-623, not the best edition, but the only one to hand.

Schleiermacher, F.D.E., *Hermeneutics: the handwritten manuscripts,* tr. James Duke and Jack Forstman, Missoula 1977, from which you will learn much less than you hoped, but something nonetheless.

Scruton, Roger, *Sexual Desire,* London and New York 1986: an attempt to vindicate the old view of sexual conduct, and the old view of marriage.

Scruton, Roger, *The Philosopher on Dover Beach,* London 1990, South Bend, Ind., 1998: a collection of essays, some of which explore further the arguments hinted at in this book – in particular the essays on Spengler and Gierke, and the essay entitled 'Man's Second Disobedience'.

Snow, C.P., *The Two Cultures and the Scientific Revolution,* Cambridge 1960, in which modern science is represented as a 'culture', to the great displeasure of Dr Leavis.

Spengler, Oswald, *The Decline of the West,* the aura of which is more effectively conveyed by its German title, *Das Untergang des Abendlandes* – the sinking of the lands of evening, 1921.

Steiner, George, *Real Presences,* London 1992, an attempt to revive, through high culture, a memory of the old religious epiphany.

Stone, Laurence, *The Family, Sex and Marriage in England, 1500–1800,* London 1977, for the history of marriage and the impact of Enlightenment ideas upon sexual conduct.

Tanner, Michael, *Wagner,* London 1996, a succinct and admiring exposition of Wagner and a debunking of the debunkers.

Till, Nicholas, *Mozart and the Enlightenment,* London 1992, a meticulous and suggestive account of the spiritual meaning of the Enlightenment.

Tönnies, Ferdinand, *Gemeinschaft und Gesellschaft*, 1887, translated as *Community and Society*, an important book which nevertheless makes you wonder whether a whole *book* was needed to make the point.

Turgenev, *Fathers and Sons,* the novel which foresaw and foresuffered all, and which proves that the literary demolition of an illusion is after all entirely futile.

Vaihinger, Hans, *The Philosophy of 'As If'*, tr. C.K. Ogden, London 1932, a book which runs many things together and which is in consequence somewhat less interesting than its title.

Van Gennep, Arnold, *Les rites de passage,* Paris 1909, first anthropological account of the process whereby early societies accomplish the transition from youth to adulthood, and from life to death.

Van Gennep, Arnold, *Religions, moeurs et légendes,* Paris 1912, for the essay on totemism.

Vico, Giambattista, *The New Science,* tr. T.G. Bergin and M.H. Fisch, Ithaca 1970, abridged (thank Heavens) but not so much as to remove all the opinionated crankiness.

Weber, Max, *Wirtschaft und Gesellschaft,* Tübingen, 1922 – selections from which have been included in all student editions of Weber. A massive attempt to describe the process of transition from traditional to modern society, in terms of the transformation of economic, social and religious ties.

Williams, Raymond, *Culture and Society 1780-1950,* London 1958, in which the culture of the 'people' is iconised, and that of the nobs tucked away out of sight. This, the founding document of 'Cultural Studies', already foretells the weaknesses that come, when a subject is built around a political agenda rather than critical analysis.

Wintle, Justin, ed., *Makers of Modern Culture,* London, 1981, a collection of biographical articles identifying leading figures in twentieth-century culture (where 'culture' includes the arts, the sciences and pop). A useful, if dated, collection, from which Wintle extracted a shorter *Dictionary of Modern Culture.* Wintle went on to compose a companion volume: *Makers of Nineteenth-Century Culture,* London 1982. The implied distinction, between modern and nineteenth-century culture, is not one that I endorse: as readers of this book will be aware, I trace modern culture to the Enlightenment, and modernism to the nineteenth century reaction against Romanticism (itself a product of Enlighten- ment).

Wittgenstein, Ludwig, *Lectures and Conversations on Aesthetics, Psychology and Religious Belief*, ed. C. Barrett, Oxford 1966, in which the greatest of modern philosophers offers valuable but unsystematic insights.

Index